MW00929820

Staying Together for at least 50 Years

For Robin,
May your love grow
ever deeper, stronger
and richer.

[signature]

Staying Together for at least 50 Years

KEEPING LOVE ALIVE FOR A LIFETIME

Lynn Parsley, MA, LPC

ISBN: 1533533180
ISBN 13: 9781533533180

To Kathleen, my partner and my best friend. Where would I be without you?

Contents

Introduction

n nearly four decades of counseling families, I have heard thousands of personal stories told by people from every walk of life. Through continuing education and mostly by experience, I have developed strategies for helping couples improve their relationships with each other, their children and their extended families. In this book I offer ideas and formulas for positive and *sustainable* change. These chapters reflect both current research on what works for couples seeking help and my own observations as a therapist. Couples have found hope and strength through trying these suggestions I have shared in our sessions. You will also find that I have referenced many other authors in the field of marriage and family counseling whose books are rich sources for additional help and understanding. What I know for sure is that when people come to counseling they want immediate practical advice they can understand and use. For troubled marriages, just talking about problems does not usually produce change. Learning new patterns of responses and behaviors makes the positive difference in resolving issues. I hope you will find these chapters to be something you can use repeatedly as a reference book for trouble-shooting and for the encouragement to see that things can truly get better.

Research has found that the main sources of marital conflict in our society are money, sex, in-laws and the division of household labor. I have written this book with these conflicts in mind. You will soon find that the chapters are meant to stand alone. They don't necessarily depend on or flow into each other even though I sometimes reference other chapters when I repeat a point. With this format you may look at the topic of a chapter and go straight to it for quick reference to pertinent solutions. I hope you will find a particular chapter to be so helpful by itself that it will be worth the purchase of the book.

Another title for this book could have been, "The Conscious, Intentional and Purposeful Marriage." You will see those three words in every chapter. I believe a couple cannot thrive without staying aware of what works for them and renewing the intention to keep doing those helpful things daily. Happy marriages require skills which are developed through practice, practice, practice. I've had many couples return after a session in which I offered clear-cut advice about changing behaviors and they say, "It didn't work." I ask, "How many times did you try it?" And they say, "Once." Such a response would send a sports coach into orbit! I hope you will read certain parts of this book over and over and try again and again to apply the principles until you get positive results.

After listening to hundreds of couples talk about their life together, I have come to one major conclusion and that is every couple wants two fundamental things: to feel supported and to have fun. My hope is that you will find in these pages ways to become aware of what works for the good of your relationship and you will be inspired to employ those practices every day for at least 50 years.

Lynn Parsley Summer, 2016

In 1981, I sometimes visited a couple who had been married for 72 years. They had spent their 92 years living in or near the little town of Fisher, Illinois. They still lived in their own home with the help of their extended family. But mainly they just took care of each other. One day I asked Grandma Hendricks, "What is the secret to staying married for over 70 years?" Mrs. Hendricks took a minute to ponder and then, as she smiled sweetly she said, "You just have to be in a good mood."

CHAPTER 1

How Did We Ever Get Together?

The author, *C.S.* Lewis, said, "No clever arrangement of bad eggs ever made a good omelet." Some people were just not meant to marry each other. They may or may not be wonderful people, but they are not wonderful as a couple. Maybe they are just too different or one partner could be one of those people who are not cut out to contribute a fair share to a positive marital experience no matter who they marry. After the initial excitement and romance in a marriage winds down, a lot of couples wonder what the original attraction was all about. One or both of the partners seem to have gotten a different person than they thought they were marrying. Their love is overshadowed by regret. Because of these factors, not all marriages can or should be saved. Yet, nearly half the marriages in our country flounder not because of a "bad match" but because couples enter their relationships ill-equipped to navigate the myriad challenges of life together. Most people in troubled marriages are not "bad eggs". They are simply lacking the tools to relate effectively. Let's start with an important part of establishing a satisfying marriage which is to learn to forgive your mate for being your opposite.

The life partner you have chosen is probably opposite from you in almost every way. You most likely have very different temperaments, habits and sexual energy. It is with shock and dismay that soon after the honeymoon you discover, "My partner is not like me!" You didn't notice or it didn't matter that you had your differences when you were in the early stages of love and commitment. For you, as with many lovers, the big revelation came after the wedding. It might take a year or two but when the truth sets in you may wonder if you have married the right person.

By the time a couple comes to me for help, each partner may have been waging vigorous campaigns to get the other person to conform to his or her own standards, preferences and ways of doing things. These campaigns have often included lecturing, criticizing and punishing. Not many couples arrive in my office saying, "We accept each other just the way we are." People say that when you get married you become "one." The problem is "which one?"

I have found that the best way to help couples stop trying to change each other is to teach them about personality types, which I refer to as temperaments. I facilitate identifying their respective types by using an uncomplicated pen and paper survey called "Wired That Way". I'll admit there are more personality inventories available out there than there are tadpoles in a frog pond. Many folks are familiar, usually through their workplace, with the Myers Briggs inventory. Others may have studied the Enneagram or filled out a form that determined what animal type they are such a dolphin or an otter. I use "Wired That Way" because Florence and Maurita Littauer, the authors of the instrument, have been writing and teaching for decades about how people's temperament types affect relationships of every kind, at home and in the workplace. There are companion books by the Littauers available which explain personality types in layman's terms and offer suggestions about personal growth and creating harmony in relationships.

One completes the "Wired That Way" inventory by checking off traits on a list of nearly 100 characteristics such as unforgiving, messy, detailed, adventurous and sunny. The results provide a portrait of strengths and weaknesses which make up one's inborn, "hard-wired" temperament. Littauer uses Aristotle's terms for the various body fluids he believed influenced a person's behaviors. The temperament types are Sanguine, Choleric, Melancholy and Phlegmatic. Popular Sanguines have never met a stranger and love to be the life of the party. They want to have fun and be involved in many different things. Powerful Cholerics are strong leaders with an innate sense of how to get things done efficiently. They are generally unemotional but have a quick temper. Perfect Melancholys love order and are idealistic. They can be critical of themselves and others, but are very loyal. Peaceful Phlegmatics are conflict avoidant and terrible procrastinators. They are observers rather than doers and have a wry sense of humor. I find it fascinating to read the detailed descriptions of the temperament types and how they affect personal attractions and interactions.

Just ask parents who have more than one child and they will tell you that each child came out of the womb bearing the traits of their individual temperament. It is truly amazing how many things about us are set from the very beginning of our lives. Understanding that no personality type is all good or all bad helps us be open to our differences. We all have our strengths and weaknesses in different categories. In marriage we fill each other's "gaps" by being opposite temperament types.

There are more than four personality types because everyone's personality consists of a blend of temperament traits from each of the four categories. Almost everyone scores heavily in two categories and lightly in the other two. The two big scores blend to indicate your type. Thus, your temperament is actually described as Choleric/Sanguine or Melancholy/Phlegmatic or one of the other several possible blends. Your temperament is always a combination of strengths and weaknesses and throughout your life your behaviors reflect these tendencies which arrived with you at birth. We may learn to adapt our behaviors as we age, but our temperament does not fundamentally change over the years. I believe that a major life task is to grow into our strengths and thus soften the rough edges of our weaknesses while maintaining our essence.

In a marriage each partner has a "go to" or "default mode" of acting and interacting which reflects the influence of temperament. People aren't generally conscious of these behavior modes because they manifest as automatically and naturally as breathing. Using a personality inventory is a great first step in helping you and your partner go from being unaware to becoming conscious of your innate differences. Often repeated marital conflicts begin to make more sense when you see that one event or conversation can be interpreted completely differently when two people with opposite temperaments are involved.

* * *

I am enthralled with the advances in neuroscience in this century. With the technologies available to brain researchers, how we think can be observed as we are engaging in thought. A Functional MRI can monitor how various areas of the brain light up or change color when they are activated. This has provided us with proof that two people can approach exactly the same task utilizing entirely different areas of their brains. Studies have shown that brain activity diversities can be attributed to such characteristics as age, gender and personality type. That is why some conversations with your mate leave you feeling that you were conversing with someone from another planet or species. His or her brain just lights up differently than yours!

When you look at all the couples you know and their personality types, you will see that most of the people married their opposite type. Have you ever noticed that messy people invariably marry neat freaks? Or that nice people marry grumpy people? Or that loud people marry quiet people? Take a minute to consider which of yours and your spouse's traits are opposite. Make note of how these differences contribute to the conflicts in your marriage. I suggest you actually write these down and look at them together. Men generally hate doing this sort of thing. Hopefully, both of you will do it because it can be fun and it often helps lead to deeper understanding. The couples I counsel actually enjoy talking over the results of "Wired That Way" as they experience quite a few "aha" moments of insight.

Pete and Jolene came for counseling because Jolene wanted Pete to help more with family responsibilities. She and Pete work full time jobs and have three school-aged children. Jolene's temperament is one of strong will, definite opinions and quick temper. Pete is a man of few words, peace loving and stubborn. Jolene wants things done "yesterday" and Pete is a procrastinator. She fusses and he retreats. You can see why they need help. Perhaps their interactions would improve if they realized that each of them could bring insights and behaviors to fit the need at hand. Opposite is not the same as wrong.

I often see couples who are opposite in multiple ways. I mostly see two people living life with two different "energies." Frequently, one partner is a "high energy" force to be reckoned with and the other has a low key energy which is at best mellow and at worst lazy. Or, one partner's energy seems to be streamlined to perfectionism and task-orientation while the other's is geared towards fun and "life as it comes." As with Pete and Jolene, there is room for both approaches in family life. It takes mutual respect and good communication to allow for each other's contributions. My mate is really good with numbers and money management. I am really good at planning fun things to do. Thus, we have money to do fun things. See how it works?

Couples sometimes tell me that the high energy spouse often feels like the "bad guy" or "the parent" and the low energy spouse feels like "the victim" or "the child." When these roles prevail in a marriage the intimate bond falls apart. It is particularly hard on the sexual bond if one spouse is feeling like he or she is being treated like a child by the other. Listen to the tone you take with each other in heated discussions. You may find yourself sounding just like one of your parents or you sound like a snarky teenager resisting control. I often hear in counseling "I hate being told what to do and how to do it!" While the other partner says "You should see it yourself and do it without having to be told." These verbal transactions are indeed parent-child communications. You can imagine that when some couples deal with conflict it can become complicated by old thoughts and feelings leftover from childhood family relationships. Talking to a spouse like a parent to a child can push some really hot buttons!

Our best hope is that we will address each other as one adult to another, keeping in mind that we can respect even if we don't prefer or replicate the other's approach to doing things. When couples agree that no personality type is inherently good or bad, they can hopefully work with each other's strengths and weaknesses more effectively. Knowing your partner's temperament characteristics helps you know what is motivating and satisfying for him or her. Instead of shaming your mate for not being more like you, a new atmosphere of mutual respect and encouragement can be developed when you see each other's differences as complementary.

Sometimes couples come for counseling who are not opposite in temperament. If two similar people get married, there are gaps in their ability to face life as a team that can cover all the bases adequately. Steven and Jenny came in for help because they felt they had lost their bond. No sex, no communication and very little cooperation left them feeling like roommates instead of mates. Their little girl was all that held them together. After doing the temperament inventory with them, it was clear that they had very similar personalities with parallel strengths and weaknesses.

Both were anxiety prone with low confidence in both decision making and assertiveness. There was no natural leader in the marriage. A lot of important things in their life together were "dead in the water" because neither of them had the life energy or skills to push towards resolution. Neither of them was good at planning and carrying out activities which would have been pleasurable and therefore bonding for them as a couple. Neither of them was trying to keep the interest alive in their marriage. They weren't succeeding in giving each other support or having fun together.

By the way, their daughter as a preschooler was already starting to parent them! This often happens when neither parent has leadership skills in the family.

I initiated Steven and Jenny's marriage counseling process by helping them understand how their temperaments contributed to their problems. This helped them to define what needed to be changed. There were behaviors that were clearly not working for them and someone in the marriage needed to "go against the grain" of their personality to get them unstuck.

In their case, I knew they needed to understand each other's fears because fear was behind much of the indecision and lack of action. I worked with them to establish conversations in which they could voice their fears and encourage each other to move forward with courage aided by one another's support. They implemented a technique I call "The Huddle," which I describe in detail in Chapter Eight. This helped them to share leadership and implement the plans they needed to run the household and have fun. They had to remain conscious and intentional about getting out of their hardwired modes of thinking and behaving in order to be an effective team.

Pete and Jolene had a deep problem with mutual respect. As John Gottman found in his research, when contempt shows up in a marriage there is a strong possibility of divorce. The parent-child interactions between Pete and Jolene were fostering contempt on a daily basis. Jolene thought her way was the best, most efficient way to get things done. Pete wanted to get it done his way and in his time. He looked at me plaintively and said "I can't do it to suit her no matter how hard I try!" Jolene expressed her feeling that, "If he loved me he would know what to do." Jolene often used shame as a weapon to get her way. Pete had established a pattern of withdrawing into stubborn silence.

"The Huddle" was a helpful tool for Pete and Jolene when Jolene let it be a discussion rather than a dictation. It was most helpful for Pete to see what he needed to contribute to the family each week and have *specific timelines* for getting things done. As long as he got things done on time, he could approach it any way he wanted to. Jolene needed to spend some time each day verbally affirming Pete for what he was doing and, most importantly, for simply who he is as a person. Pete is a kind, funny and perceptive guy. If Jolene would allow herself to receive feedback from Pete she could learn to loosen up, have more fun and communicate acceptance to others, especially their children. They began to relate to each other adult to adult and, once in a while, Jolene even let her inner child come out to play.

* * *

Another way to examine your differences is through the "Imago" theory of Dr. Harville Hendrix. His premise is that you are most strongly attracted to a person who possesses characteristics which will interact with yours to create the problems you had with your mother and father growing up. The idea is that we are wounded, usually unintentionally, by our parents through their personality traits, their career and lifestyle choices and/or their parenting patterns. Our parents' inner pain and struggles may have overflowed on us in many ways as we lived with them. We always carry the feelings generated by our interactions with our parents into our adult relationships. Hendrix's theory is that we are most attracted to a person who will give us another chance to "win" or "master" the issues we had with our mother and father.

This powerful draw to a potential mate is referred to by Dr. Jeff Auerbach in his book "Irritating the Ones You Love" as the "invisible connection" because it happens totally in our unconscious. We are drawn, like a moth to flame, to pair up with someone that will trigger our deepest pain. Because the early stages of love are so exhilarating, we are blinded to the inevitable problems that lie ahead. Only through the conscious examination of our childhood history can we uncover what our conflicts were. Some common parent-child issues are abandonment, guilt manipulation and unreliability. When we become aware of our sensitive areas of stored up pain, we can make conscious choices to behave in thoughtful, effective ways when conflicts with our mate arise.

* * *

Let's get back to how our brains are wired in ways that may cause a couple to react in opposite, even opposing, ways. As I mentioned earlier, there have been brain function studies supporting the idea that males and females usually have some fundamentally different brain reactions which are gender related and supported by social convention. Indeed, women are more geared towards the maintenance of relationships and are encouraged in that ability while men are often more focused on accomplishments outside of the home. Men process language and communication differently from women. Of course there are exceptions to these generalities. Perhaps from generation to generation, as roles in society change, the DNA and brain activity differences will diminish. Even though gender differences have been proven to exist, it has been my observation that most differences affecting relationships stem from the couple's personality types being opposite. Our inborn temperament even dictates the *way* we love.

Dr. Gary Chapman's book "The Five Love Languages" explains that there are ways human beings like to give and receive love which are pretty much life-long preferences. You will find references to this concept of "love languages" in other chapters of this book because it is so profoundly influential in happy families. Our love languages are the ways we communicate love through behaviors. Dr. Chapman says that people show love through the giving of gifts, touch, words of affirmation, spending quality time together and through acts of service. His book includes a "test" that will help each of you identify your primary love language.

Many couples come to counseling because one or both of the partners are feeling lonely in their marriage. They don't *feel* loved. As we look at each person's temperament and then survey their love language preferences, we see the "opposites attract" principle at the root of their loneliness. Remember the Golden Rule that says, "Do unto others as you would have them do unto you?" Well, the better rule for marriage and for all relationships is, "Do unto others as *they* would have you do unto *them*." Loving another person meaningfully begins with understanding what *they* feel to be loving behavior, with what *their* love language is. We must be conscious and intentional to move out of our tendencies to do what *we* like and become comfortable with loving according to our *mate's* needs, likes and dislikes. The importance of doing this every day is why some people say that marriage takes a lot of work.

We may marry our opposite and experience all of the trouble this generates, but remember that when we are opposite we have the ways to complement and join each other in deeply intimate ways. Try to keep a sense of humor about your differences and practice gratitude about what your mate contributes to the quality of your lives together. Variety *is* the spice of life!

CHAPTER 2

The Sacred Space

hy is there such a high rate of infidelity in America? How can you protect your marriage from this assault on the soul of your union? The answer is simple but not easy: you have to value fidelity with such certainty that the effort and commitment needed to preserve it will seem a worthy investment.

Truth be known, not many people actually believe it is possible to have sex with only your mate "for as long as you both shall live." Almost every couple enters marriage with a "we will be faithful" attitude but have no specific plans as to how to support the original aim of fidelity. Sadly, more things will naturally come along to pull a person into an affair than will to keep him or her faithful. As with many aspects of marriage, fidelity is preserved by conscious, deliberate effort.

Research indicates that a frequently cited reason people give for cheating is because they are lonely in their marriage. "My wife doesn't understand me!" has been a standard pick-up line for centuries. It is often true, especially at certain stages of family life, that a spouse may not be getting important needs met. Feeling deprived emotionally and/or sexually is an early warning signal of vulnerability to an affair. Job one in preventing an affair is maintaining a close bond with your mate in which your emotional and sexual needs are met. However, I believe there is another compelling reason why we are tempted to stray.

Human beings are animals. Sexuality is chemistry-based. Hormones, pheromones and neurotransmitters fuel the flames of desire. Attraction can begin with a kind word or deed, but it can also begin with a glance or a whiff of perfume. In a lifetime one can have magic with multiple people in any number of circumstances.

Here's the thing: initial attraction is very exciting for primitive reasons. The chemical activated in your brain in the early stages of love is phenylethylamine, or PEA. It is an opiate-like substance which has the same exhilarating effect as cocaine. Life is good when PEA is coursing through your brain! Your senses seem keener, your step is livelier and you feel happy. All this generates an overwhelming "urge to merge" with the person associated with such a high.

When we are in this state of mind everything else pales in comparison, especially the mundane daily grind of married life. "Old love" can't hold a candle to "new love." An affair is captivating simply *because it is new.* However, researchers believe PEA chemistry can be sustained between the same two people for no more than 18 to 24 months. If that couple stays together after PEA subsides, the PEA is replaced long term by oxytocin. Oxytocin makes humans feel bonded and nurturing towards one another. Women produce it more readily than men, but men have it, too. Oxytocin, along with some other brain chemicals such as dopamine, certainly is a forger of marital bonds, yet it lacks the fireworks of PEA. PEA may inspire you to take wedding vows but it doesn't last to keep you faithful to your marriage partner in the long run.

Fidelity remains possible only if, when you feel "the tingles" with someone outside of your marriage, you think "Uh oh!" rather than, "Oh boy!" It is one thing to be reminded that you are a sexually alive human being. It is another to believe that an impulse is a command to be obeyed. Faithfulness is in serious trouble if there is no impulse control because the impulses will inevitably come over the lifetime of a marriage.

What is marriage? Hopefully it is more than just the legal recognition of a commitment between two people to stay together for a lifetime. We may regard a wedding as a ceremony of promise between two bonded souls. At its best, a wedding is an outward expression of the inner spiritual reality of the relationship. Ideally, it reflects a union of hearts which has already occurred, which is why some couples never bother with a ceremony. Maybe many marriages don't last because there was never an inner spiritual reality of union before, during or after the wedding. Florence Littauer writes that "After every wedding comes a marriage." It seems to be the case that wedding fantasies are far grander than marriage realities.

I personally believe marriage, whether it is formalized or not, is an agreement between two people to be each other's primary source of emotional closeness, companionship and financial support. It is usually a promise to be each other's only source of sexual intimacy. It is a covenant to maintain together a "sacred space" into which no one else may enter.

A good way to convey this idea of sacred space is by looking at concentric circles. Each circle represents how close or distant someone is relative to you and your partner in the center circle, with the largest circle being the least intimate. In the outermost ring you will find a stranger you see on the street or a neighbor you know by sight but not by name. As the circles get smaller they contain the folks you know well and care about. The smallest circles include friends and extended family. The one next to the center is where your children belong. The innermost circle, the center, is the sacred space. You and your mate keep your union there.

In recent decades, our culture has shifted towards couples putting their children in the center circle. This often means that one or the other spouse is relegated to the second circle. This is a big mistake. I firmly believe the greatest gift a couple can give their children is a good, stable and enduring marriage. Our children's security is built on the quality of their parents' relationship. If special emphasis is put on keeping the sacred space for only the two of you, you'll have a marriage that is strengthened by that profound intimacy, and divorce is not the likely outcome. The children want and need you two to stay together!

The conclusions reached through decades of research on the effects of divorce on child development are irrefutable. Children of divorce suffer negative consequences which often extend into their adult lives, especially in relationships. Granted, there are marriages so very toxic that the fallout is worse for the children's well-being than the effects of divorce would be. Children learn what they live. We can see this in the generational patterns of violence, addiction, and, yes, infidelity. Not every marriage should be preserved for the sake of the children. If your marriage is not poison to you and your children, let your children be an inspiration for you to remain faithful to your mate.

If you are to maintain the "sacred space" in your marriage, it is vital to have in your home a "sacred place". Your bedroom is that place, your sanctuary. Your children need to learn from day one that they can only enter your bedroom by permission. You close your bedroom door when you want privacy. You lock the door at night so your children have to knock before entering. Baby monitors give you auditory access to their needs without their needs interfering with yours.

A married couple's sacred space can be intruded upon by having a child regularly sleep in their bed. I am dismayed by the number of times couples have admitted in counseling that this has been a big deterrent to their sex life. I have also heard many times that couples sleep with their pets. I knew a couple who let five dogs onto their bed each night. That's not only a deterrent to sex, it is a detriment to sleep!

* * *

There is much more to preserving your sacred space than making sure your children don't enter it. We guard our sacred space with our minds as well as our actions. Fantasizing about someone you actually know is an initial step down the path to an affair. Once you know you feel attracted to someone other than your partner (remember PEA?), your inclination is to try to be alone with that person to talk to him or her as frequently as possible. Therefore, in order to protect yourself from an affair, you have to make exact plans in your mind for avoiding contact with the person you are drawn to. Contact is kerosene on the embers of attraction, but conscious avoidance lets things cool off. Unfueled fires eventually die out.

Plans to avoid the person you desire should address all levels of one-on-one communication and in-person contact. If you have to be in contact with the person either socially or in the workplace, keep it short and simple. Don't share personal and family information directly with him or her. Don't go out for drinks or find a reason to call, text or email "after hours." If you have to travel with this person for any reason, it is important that you stay sober, keep conversations "on the surface" and call your spouse as often as or even more often than usual. Whatever you do, DO NOT TELL THE PERSON YOU DESIRE THAT YOU ARE ATTRACTED!

Some men and women have told me that talking to a very trusted friend who values fidelity as much as they do has been helpful. This is a method of accountability that works if you will actually tell your friend the ongoing truth about what you are thinking and doing and they will actually provide an honest response. Look at how many famous figures surrounded themselves with people who would collude to promote their adultery rather than challenge it. You are better served by true friends who won't always agree with you when you are tempted to stray.

If someone is flirting with or actively pursuing you, you must overcome the emotional rush that comes packaged with such an ego boost. Who cannot be moved by special attention and flattery? The worst thing you can do is say to yourself, "I'll just enjoy this and see what happens, but I will know where to draw the line." Hello! Lines don't get drawn when your primitive brain takes over.

People tell me in counseling, "It just happened!" You can be sure that whatever happened involved a series of decisions that led to actually having extra-marital sex. Good decisions in the beginning of attraction will prevent poor decisions compelled by chemistry and emotions later on.

Sometimes an affair develops over days and weeks of going "one step further." For others, sex in the utility closet at work is supposedly the result of the two people "just" indulging simultaneous urges while having little or no emotional connection. I've had clients tell me, "It wasn't an affair, it was only sex. It doesn't hurt my relationship with my partner because I'm not in love with someone else."

I remind these sexual adventurers that it might not be "just sex" to the other person involved or to their mate. When two people experience an orgasm together, powerful brain chemicals are released. Dopamine and oxytocin foster pleasure and emotional bonding which by-pass your rational mind. One part of your brain may think, "This isn't an affair," but another part of your brain is shouting, "Yes it is!"

Unemotional trysts as well as affairs can result in pregnancy, disease, blackmail or homicide, even when, for one or both of the two involved, it was "just sex." For instance, I've known many wives who found out their husbands were unfaithful by way of a phone call or visit from the "other woman" who was trying to stake her claim or by finding out at their annual physical that they have a sexually transmitted disease.

Let me just say, if you own a communication device of any kind and you are having an affair, it is only a matter of time before you are BUSTED. Computer experts can even find history of activity you thought you deleted. Cell phone records are easily accessed and text messages have been the beginning of the end of many marriages in this decade! There are books and videos out now with instructions on how to tell if someone is lying (and cheating). The combination of basic intuition and modern technology leaves very few infidels undetected.

That being said, your primary responsibility is to guard your own actions, not to police your partner's. However, keeping quiet when things don't seem right may be a missed opportunity to prevent the worst from happening. I always say, "If you don't acknowledge something, it can't be fixed."

Being sexually attracted outside of your marriage, or suspecting that your partner is, can best be handled by doubling your efforts to create closeness with your spouse. Take inventory of your current level of marital intimacy, both emotional and sexual. When was the last time you had fun together? How long has it been since you spiced things up in the bedroom or even made known your desire to do so? Have you been consistently concentrating on intentionally filling your partner's love tank? The honest answers to these questions are the best gauge of how vulnerable your marriage is to an affair.

Every love guru suggests that couples keep their marriages alive and well by regularly going on dates. If nothing else, the fact that you go out for special time together signals to each other, your children, extended family, neighbors and co-workers that you highly value your relationship. Some of those people need to be convinced of your devotion to each other so they will respect the boundaries surrounding your sacred space. Along that same line, keep pictures of your loved ones close at hand and speak positively about your family in the presence of other people. These serve as reminders to yourself and others of what is truly important to you, especially when temptation arrives.

If the laws of physics apply to relationships, and I believe they do, we can expect every marriage to deteriorate into complete ruins because of entropy (the gradual decline of everything into disorder and uselessness). Only if a couple is consciously, intentionally and purposefully devoted to preserving their sacred space can they form a force stronger than the entropy that would pull them apart. Fidelity is a choice, a choice you'll make over and over in the span of your married life. Faithfulness is most possible when you actually plan for it rather than simply hoping it will all work out somehow.

* * *

Jeff called me to set up counseling because Allie had asked him to move out after seven years of marriage. Allie thought some of Jeff's stories about where he'd been and what he'd been doing didn't add up. Allie did what any 21st century wife would do. She searched through his computer and cell phone for activity she couldn't recognize as legitimate. She found what she was looking for.

Jeff and Allie had a two-year-old daughter who was the focus of Allie's energies. Jeff often felt like the odd man out in the family circle. He knew that their daughter was always Allie's top priority, bar none. The child even slept in the bed with them most nights. Jeff was missing Allie's attention even more than he realized.

Jeff and Allie met Karen and Chip in their Sunday school class and thought they were a nice, happy couple. However, in reality, Karen experienced Chip as primarily devoted to his job, thinking about work even when he was home. She perceived that Chip only half listened to her while he browsed texts and emails. When they could have had time together he chose to play golf or watch football. Contrary to their public image as the perfect couple, they were not feeling close to each other at all.

Meanwhile, Jeff and Karen became better acquainted as they served on a Sunday school class committee with a few other class members to plan the annual Sweetheart Banquet. The two of them formed a connection through easy conversation and a certain tingle of excitement between them. It felt good. They decided they should meet for lunch to discuss details of the banquet. They gave each other undivided attention. It felt good. They hugged and kissed. It felt good. Jeff and Karen could barely remember feeling so exhilarated with their mates. It all just felt so good...until they were caught.

It wasn't until Allie told Jeff their marriage was over that he thought about all he would lose in a divorce. Chip was still clueless about Karen's unfaithfulness, but she was willing to confess and leave him for Jeff. Jeff's choice was to try to save his marriage. When I met him, Jeff was feeling terrible about hurting Karen and was grieving over the loss of his relationship with her. Salvaging his marriage was going to be a painful, arduous endeavor. I was glad he and Allie came for help.

Choosing a marriage counselor should be undertaken as carefully as investing in a house or buying a car. Whether or not you find a skilled marriage counselor could make or break the outcome of counseling. Start by interviewing various counselors on the phone or in person to find out about their level of experience, their history of dealing effectively with the problems you will be presenting, and what methods of counseling they utilize.

For instance, I believe if a marriage counselor doesn't give "homework assignments" as a standard practice, very little permanent progress will be achieved. Saving a marriage is a seven-day-a-week effort. Just talking to a therapist for an hour a week, or even less often, is not enough. Each time the couple returns my first question is "What's better, what's worse, what's the same?" With that we analyze what new thoughts and behaviors are working or what is keeping them stuck in the old self-defeating patterns.

When it comes to helping a couple overcome the devastation of infidelity, many counselors, especially clergy, are not comfortable with and/or skilled in dealing with the profound anger and despair the offended spouse is feeling. Most often, when a couple has been wounded by one or both partner's unfaithfulness and seeks counseling, the partners are only marginally hopeful that they can work it out. Maintaining a vision of hope for the reparation of the marriage when the partners are feeling sad, mad and discouraged is a major gift a counselor can give. Counseling helps the couple keep going when it feels too hard to try.

* * *

In my approach, the marriage is my client, not either of the individuals. When the couple and I engage in marriage counseling, everything we do is a three-person team effort directed towards strengthening the relationship. Raising awareness of problems and solutions and eliciting open accountability are goals to reach in counseling. In my work with Jeff and Allie, the foremost goal was to heal their marriage by achieving forgiveness.

Forgiveness is the foundation upon which a new and better relationship can be built. It involves the cleaning and disinfecting of emotional wounds. Sometimes counselors rush their clients through the forgiveness stage of reconciliation. I think that a less-than-thorough effort regarding forgiveness is like stitching the surface of an infected cut. What breeds beneath those stitches cannot be healthy. I more thoroughly explain the process of forgiveness in Chapter 3.

* * *

I spent one of the initial sessions alone with Allie allowing her to express her anger without inhibition. I wanted to prepare her for a joint session in which she would honestly present to Jeff her feelings about the affair. Allie was typically uncomfortable with expressing anger to another person for fear of hurting their feelings or "rocking the boat." Conversely, a part of her wanted to make Jeff hurt the way she was hurting. It was helpful for Allie to learn that her ambivalence about anger as well as her desire for Jeff to suffer for hurting her is a normal human reaction to emotional pain.

Additionally, Allie wanted to confront Karen for her part in the affair. In dealing with adultery, confronting both parties who were involved is not always a bad idea. Talking to Karen would have been a way for Allie to reestablish the boundaries around her relationship with Jeff. I suggested that Allie write a letter to Karen and go over it with me before sending it. This would ensure that she expressed herself clearly and did not communicate threats. I did not advocate an in-person attempt to talk because of how quickly it could deteriorate into an ugly scene. A letter would be much more dignified.

After meeting with Allie, I then had a session with Jeff to instruct him in how to react to Allie's anger. I told him he must not give excuses and rationalizations for his behavior. Rather he must keep acknowledging that he was wrong and deserved the anger Allie felt and finally would direct towards him. He had to validate her pain by verbally expressing empathy and remorse. A "forgiveness session" is not a time for defensiveness. Dr. Gary Chapman's book "The Five Languages of Apology" is a helpful guide for achieving forgiveness at this stage of counseling. Just saying "I'm sorry" is rarely enough to smooth things out.

I discouraged Allie from trying to solicit graphic details about the liaisons. I believe there are some pictures you just don't want in your head. It is human nature to want the specific details associated with a trauma (and adultery is a trauma). We think the more details we have, the more we can make sense of it all. Rather than helping Allie gather details about the affair, I assisted her in achieving forgiveness for Jeff by facilitating the development of two major assurances from him. After she had fully expressed her anger to Jeff, these assurances were the next part of helping her move through the healing.

The first of the needed assurances for Allie was that Jeff, through self-examination and our discussions in counseling, had achieved complete awareness of all the factors which contributed to his unfaithful behavior. This included understanding how he overcame his inner obstacles such as a moral conscience and/or a fear of negative consequences. Simply put, Allie needed to know that Jeff had come to understand why it happened. For Jeff and Allie, as with many (but not all) couples, destructive factors existed both inside of Jeff and within the marriage itself and are likely still present when marriage counseling begins. Pinpointing these things is the foundation of building a new and better relationship after an affair.

The second assurance Allie needed was that Jeff was learning helpful skills and was committed to utilizing every possible means to prevent another affair. It took many sessions for this to be achieved because Jeff needed several sessions to learn all these things about himself and how to restore their bond, and it took several sessions for Allie to be convinced he'd learned them. Allie also needed to look at herself and their marriage, especially at how she had let their daughter into the sacred space.

* * *

I explained to both of them a concept I call "knots." Knots are the feelings in the pit of your stomach that you associate with incidents of fear or pain. For instance, if you are in an auto accident at an intersection you may feel knots every time you approach an intersection for months or even years after the accident. If your spouse is a recovering alcoholic who used to come home late after drinking in bars, you will have knots every time he is late coming home for a long time after he quits drinking. Knots are not formed in the conscious part of your brain. They are classically conditioned responses associated with noxious stimuli. I explained to Allie and Jeff that Allie would have knots regarding any of Jeff's behaviors that might remind her of the affair. Coming home late from work, secretiveness or even going to the church where he met Karen can activate knots.

The best cure for knots is the passing of time without anything associated with the knots happening again. Jeff had to keep his nose clean in every way for many, many months before Allie's knots loosened. Meanwhile, Jeff needed to establish a high level of accountability by allowing Allie access to his personal information. She had to have the means to see his texts, emails and history of phone calls. Jeff needed to keep a predictable schedule and let Allie know where he was at any given time. This may sound intrusive and a harsh price to pay for being unfaithful, but accountability is what it takes to restore trust and release knots.

I have found that a betrayed spouse will indeed, and for a good long while, check communication devices and her mate's whereabouts. However, there seems to be a natural shelf life for this need to keep checking. The time it takes to reach the point of no longer wanting to check is unique to the individual, but it does eventually become wearisome and unnecessary if all else is going well. It took tremendous patience and non-defensiveness on Jeff's part to endure this stage of reconciliation. He had to see this level of openness as one of the major ways he was making amends for what he had done. He found that his patience ultimately paid off. We spent our final sessions discussing ways to make their relationship stronger than ever and their commitment to the marriage was renewed.

Yes, there was healing and reconciliation for Jeff and Allie and for many other couples who have suffered from infidelity. There have been several books written to aid in restoring the emotional and sexual relationship for a couple who have weathered an affair. "After The Affair" (2nd Edition) by Janis Spring, PhD is a particularly good one. Restoration of intimacy and trust is the zenith of repairing the damage of infidelity. My hope is that you will always consciously and intentionally guard your sacred space with all your might and reap the joys of a secure and trusting marriage "until death do you part."

CHAPTER 3

Forgive For Goodness Sake

ark Twain said, "Forgiveness is the fragrance the violet sheds on the heel that crushes it." Someone else said, "Forgiveness is when you take your hands off his throat." No matter how we define it, we know that forgiving is not an easy thing to do. We have to appeal to our higher nature to get past the very human desire to see the people who have wronged us suffer and pay for what they did. Our pain can cause us to simply hold a grudge or plot a terrible revenge. Unforgiveness is at the root of a lot of dysfunction in a marriage. Holding on to pain and anger in a relationship is a log jam in the river of love. A lot of crap backs up behind it, undermining any hope of one's being closely bonded to their mate.

Not being able to forgive someone is a ball and chain around your own ankle. It is more toxic to you than to the person you can't forgive. It's like **you** eat rat poison and wait for the rat to die. I believe failing to forgive causes physical and mental health problems for millions of people. It will almost certainly ruin a marriage.

As I have listened to my clients talk about their unwillingness to forgive, I learned that those folks were subject to some misconceptions about forgiveness that kept them stuck. Perhaps you struggle with some of the same misconceptions.

One of the biggest misconceptions about forgiveness is that if you forgive a person you are saying that what they did is okay. You are afraid if you forgive them you would be discounting and invalidating all of your hurt or outrage. It would be like saying, "My feelings don't matter." What is true about forgiveness is that when you are in pain due to being wronged, you need very much for your feelings to be validated and met with compassion.

Another objection to forgiveness made by people who have been aggrieved is that forgiveness is the same as reconciliation and automatic renewal of a relationship with the offending person. This fear is especially present in men and women who have suffered abuse, neglect, humiliation, betrayal and/or rejection by someone they trusted. They have no intention of ever being in the same room with the abuser much less allowing them to get close again.

Mary Ann was only 12 years old when her male cousin, Ted, forced her to perform oral sex on him. Because her family and his family were often together at their grandparents' farm, Ted had opportunities to abuse Mary Ann many times before he left home and stopped attending family gatherings. The trauma of being molested followed Mary Ann into her adult life with negative consequences to her mental health and her relationships. As she told me her story she started with "I have never told anyone about this." We worked together through many sessions of anguish as the healing began for Mary Ann in counseling.

As Mary Ann began to accept that the sexual abuse was not her fault and she could "take her power back" from Ted after all these years, I brought up the subject of forgiveness. I explained that forgiving Ted would actually set *her* free from the bitterness she harbored. If she could forgive him, she would be able to permanently close the box that held her abuse memories. The idea of forgiving Ted was unacceptable to Mary Ann when I brought it up. She declared, "I have avoided him for all these years. There is no way I can see him or talk to him ever again!"

I carefully explained that she could forgive Ted without confronting him or contacting him in any way. She could address him in my office as if he were sitting there or she could write a letter she would never send to pour out her anger and pain. After all, this was a process for setting *her* free rather than trying to establish a relationship with someone who hurt her so badly. She wasn't very sure I was leading her in the right direction, but she gave it a try. She wrote a scathing letter to Ted saying all she had ever wanted to say to him. At the end she said she was ready to let it all go. After we processed the letter together, Mary Ann admitted that she felt "a thousand pounds lighter." Remember this happened after we had done a great deal of healing work. It is unreasonable to think that people can forgive the people who hurt them without working their way up to it. Yet, I have had the privilege of helping people come to this liberation of forgiveness and not many things I do is more powerful.

* * *

A lot of people carry pain caused by a loved one (or a stranger or an acquaintance) for decades without telling a single soul about what happened. As with Mary Ann, telling the story of hurt is the beginning of healing and, ultimately, forgiving the perpetrator is liberating for the victim even if the offender is dead. We can forgive someone without ever telling them in person. For whatever the reason, the person may not be available to hear it. Do it anyway. It frees your soul and makes room for love, joy and peace to dwell where the hurt has been locked up. Learning to forgive also teaches you how to receive forgiveness for your own mistakes.

I have also had folks tell me they can't forgive because they cannot or do not want to forget. They feel that if forgiveness requires forgetting, they will be left vulnerable to future transgressions. Others say they can't forget because the memories are just too vivid. This is one reason I do not encourage couples to go into detail about infidelities. As noted in Chapter Two, I tell them, "There are some pictures you just do not want in your head." At any rate, remembering what happened is an effect of trauma that most people do not fully overcome. Some parts of remembering are essential to our survival as human beings. Forgetting is not essential to forgiving. However, you don't get to keep bringing it up once you offer forgiveness.

If forgiveness is not the same as saying it is okay, or that you are willing to be close again or that you can forget, then what is it? I believe forgiveness is when you stop dwelling on the negative thoughts and feelings associated with the person who hurt you. You stop storing resentment in a box *you frequently open.*

Mostly, forgiveness is about letting go of your desire to have the other person pay for what they did according to how and when you want them to pay. It is releasing the transgressor to be dealt with by their conscience or God or the universe or karma. You must say to yourself that you are no longer attached to the outcome. Forgiveness is easier if you remember that you are not perfect and that you are glad you did not always get a harsh punishment when you hurt someone. Mercy is **not** getting what you deserve! Mercy and forgiveness are often closely entwined.

* * *

I want to give you some guidelines for approaching a person you feel has done you wrong so that there can be a resolution of the conflict. No one should have ever said that it is nobler to suffer in silence than it is to have your say when something negative and of magnitude has occurred. Hopefully, these guidelines will give you the courage and power to move forward in getting things settled.

In your marriage, talking through the pain or anger you feel is vital to the health of your relationship if the offense is something you can't ignore. Nitpicking on a daily basis is not what I am talking about. Some spouses are so habitually critical that it is hard for their mate to listen when something really matters. Keep your complaining to a minimum and you will be heard when you speak up. It is important to remember that when you are addressing the real injuries, timing is important. Sooner is better when getting things out in the open. However, make sure you are not still flooded with emotion before you make your approach. Take time to cool off and think through what you want to say and how to say it. It would probably serve you well to write it down or at least make notes before you start the conversation with your mate.

Here's the outline for how to present your complaint to your partner.

1. Say specifically what was done that hurt or angered you. Stick to one thing rather than recounting every problem that occurred since you met.
2. Say how it made you feel. This can include how it impacted your self- esteem and your ability to trust.
3. Say how it affected your life. For instance, it made you late for work or your checks bounced.
4. Say what your mate can do to make it right. This can include asking for a statement of real empathy, a verbal apology and/or an action.
5. Say how you want things to be between you in the future. This could be anything from "I hope to start communicating more clearly" to "I want to end the relationship." At best, you may say, "Let's make a fresh start."

Now that you have thought about what you want to say to your mate, take time to prepare your heart to approach the conversation with a reconciliatory tone rather than a tone of accusation and anger. Think about your love for your partner and about what you know is an approach that works with him or her when engaging in serious conversations, and what doesn't work. Plan to start with some affirmations of what has been good between you and/or some virtue you appreciate about your mate. Then start the conversation with a statement that begins with "I" rather than "you".

When the pain is deep and the transgression has caused a serious breach in the relationship, having a professional counselor assist you with this process could be very helpful. A counselor can help a couple stay on the subject and remain calm during the discussion. I try to help couples stay in the conversation and see it through to its conclusion even when it is hard to keep going.

So many people suffer in silence for years and years because they are averse to conflict. They are afraid that if they talk about their hurt or anger it will cause a fight or even end the relationship. A counselor can mediate the discussion to avert a fight and help all complaints to be aired. Just remember that holding everything in can make you sick and destroy your marriage.

* * *

I have learned that a person can offer forgiveness much more readily if the offender makes a sincere and meaningful apology. There are several elements to an effective apology. These are some of the best to employ.

A good apology begins with accepting responsibility for your behavior. This is the opposite of blaming others or making excuses for what you did. You are not saying it was your intention to negatively impact the other person, but that you did it and it was offensive. Remember, perception is reality when it comes to your loved one's feelings about what happened. Your partner's feelings about it *do not have to make sense to you* in order for you to own up and make an apology.

After taking responsibility, you absolutely must express empathy about how what you did made the other person feel. Acknowledge the impact of what you have done. Never, ever say "You shouldn't feel that way." Nor should you say "I am sorry, but..." Surely you know that when you say "but" in the middle of a sentence you wipe out everything that came before it. You can gain a lot of ground by saying "I can see you were very hurt by what I did." The more accurately you can express empathy the more likely you will receive the forgiveness.

An apology is best if you say what flaw in yourself led to your injurious action. This is not to sound like an excuse but rather it should convey true self-reflection and insight. It should demonstrate that you know how the offense happened so you can guard against repeating it. You may need to say something like, "I am not paying careful enough attention to you when you talk to me." The worst thing a person can do when trying to apologize is blame the other person for one's own behavior. In one instance, for example, a client called Josh told his wife Amber that he would never have used the credit card to buy his sound system without discussing it with her if she were not so "tight with money". She did not hear an apology in that statement!

The best apology ends with the statement of a plan to not offend again. You can solicit an opinion from your partner as to how you can avoid doing this behavior again. Such a plan indicates more concretely that you take responsibility for your actions and you want to make amends by doing better. Josh, for example, promised Amber he would make no purchases of more than $100.00 without discussing it with her first. Her trust was rebuilt when he followed through with his promise. If your mate receives a really good apology, forgiveness can be given and trust can be restored, too.

When a partner fails to forgive, there is a greater likelihood that he or she will only see the negative in their mate and in the relationship. Unforgiveness becomes a filter that prevents anything good and positive from being consciously accepted. Forty-year-old Ellen made up her mind that her husband, Ron, was selfish and insensitive because he criticized her cooking and housekeeping early in their marriage. She never discussed how his criticism hurt her and so Ron persisted in the insults obliviously and never apologized. Years later she was continually gathering evidence to support her theory that her husband is a jerk. She ignored anything that might indicate otherwise. What a miserable way to live! Their marriage is collapsing under the weight of it.

If you are not feeling close to your mate, look deep inside yourself and search your heart to see if you have failed to forgive. You may find a trove of "little things" that have mounted up or there may be one or two major offenses you never got over. If you wish for a marriage in which you have pleasure and lots of support and closeness, then you must try to keep the slate clean with your partner. You are forgiving even when you have been deeply hurt because you want love to prevail.

CHAPTER 4

The Pause Button on the Remote Control

This chapter is about communication. It is about how to talk to each other as an aspect of enjoying being with each other. Most couples will admit that talking is not the primary way they bond. They bond mostly by being present to each other in times of need and in sharing pleasurable activities. You want to be close to your mate? Give support and have fun! Like it or not, fostering these two aspects of your relationship does include having conversations.

We have a variety of conversations with our partners. Hopefully, most of those conversations are means of giving support and having fun. Some conversations are meant to draw a couple into each other's world of thoughts and experiences. Some are "business meetings". Some are attempts to resolve conflict and hurt feelings. Regardless of what it is we are talking about, the conversation will go better if we have two things: willingness and skill.

Because so many people marry their opposite personality type and for most of us, the opposite gender, you can be sure that one of you likes to talk and one of you prefers not to, as in "I'd rather have a root canal." Belief in gender differences has been exaggerated in our culture for decades, but one that is supported by research is that women enjoy talking as an integral part of a relationship more than men do. Men particularly hate conversations that make them feel guilty or inadequate. When they feel they are being disrespected or criticized they clam up. A woman can dislike talking if she feels threatened or anxious while communicating with her partner. For many females, feeling threatened in a conversation is not about physical violence but about the safety and future of the relationship. They would rather not talk if it is going to make them feel insecure about being faithfully loved.

"How to Improve Your Marriage without Talking About It" by Dr. Patricia Love offers effective guidelines for avoiding the pitfall of inciting shame and fear in marital communications. John M. Gottman, PhD. has done decades of research with couples to determine how some marriages stay together and others fall apart. His book, "The Seven Principles for Making Marriage Work" reveals the wisdom he garnered from videotaping couples' interactions and following up for years afterward to see which marriages lasted. By observing their patterns of communication he could, often within ten minutes or less, predict which marriages would fail.

Dr. Love and Dr. Gottman offer in their respective books theories and advice about communication based on their research studies and years of counseling couples. I recommend their books as in-depth tools for helping your marriage. After nearly four decades of observing couples in my practice, I have to agree with the research done by various experts who found that it is not only what you say but also how you say it that makes a difference in the outcome of a conversation.

Most of us learned our communication styles in childhood. We usually do with our spouses what our parents did or didn't do with each other. Also, if a child is traumatized in some way it may affect his or her adult relationships, especially in being able to share on a vulnerable level about needs and feelings. Things from our childhood that affect our present relationships are commonly referred to as "baggage". Some of us arrive in our marriage with the Samsonite stuffed full!

There is a saying, "To know all is to forgive all." In a marriage, if you know all about your mate's inner influences including the baggage, you can be more compassionate when he or she disappoints you. A huge part of communicating well with your partner is not taking things that are said or not said as being intended deliberately to hurt you. It is a fact that very few of us are skilled communicators even after we have been instructed in the ways of effective communication. Our clumsiness with words can hurt a loved one unintentionally. If you feel injured by something your mate said it is helpful to ask, in a genuinely curious not accusative tone of voice, "What did you mean by that?"

I believe it is very helpful for couples to talk about their growing up years with each other so the baggage can be identified before it sabotages the relationship. I have already described in Chapter One how your personality type affects your approach to relationships, including your style of communication. It is equally important to be aware of the models of conversation you each observed in your respective families. My Norwegian partner says you can hear a pin drop during her family's Thanksgiving dinners as my relatives talk over each other and compete to tell the best story at ours. Some of my clients say they did not observe their parents having many conversations at all. Others say they never once heard their parents argue. And then there are lots of us who heard our first cuss words when our parents were fighting. The problems do not lie in whether our families had arguments. The problems lie in **how** they argued and, more importantly, *how they made up.*

* * *

As you may recall from Chapter One, Jake and Jillian agreed to go to a marriage counselor because they couldn't talk without fighting.

Jake felt that a conversation with Jillian was really her opportunity to nag him about what he was failing to do to help around the house. Jillian wanted to feel closer and more supported by Jake but she ultimately resorted to criticizing him for his shortcomings.

When they sought help, the counselor led them through a commonly employed technique called "active listening". The counselor taught them to each say something that felt important and the other would reflect back what he or she heard. Jillian could say "I get angry when you leave your shoes in the family room and I have to pick them up." Jake learned to reply "You feel mad when I leave my shoes lying around." These exercises worked well in the office to help them hear each other. However, even though this technique can be helpful in many efforts to talk in everyday life, researchers have found that most couples are not likely to discuss things this way. When Jake got home he still said "Move the shoes your own damn self." If counseling about successful conversational techniques fails to go deeper than "active listening," it will rarely be successful.

I think every couple is capable of finding a style of resolving conflict that works for them. It is important to remember that all couples argue, sometimes loudly, and arguing is not a sign of a bad marriage. The essential factor is how quickly the participants get over it. How soon can the two of you clear the air and enjoy each other's company again? For most of us, part of getting over an argument quickly has a lot to do with what is said and done during it. Keep in mind the best way to be happy together is to give support and have fun together. Even difficult conversations can facilitate these goals if both of you are trying to be effective communicators through guarding what you say and how you say it. Here are some guidelines to help achieve the goals of giving support and having fun together by talking to each other.

* * *

I will start with the foundation principle of a good marriage. The principle is that you must each be conscious, intentional and purposeful about taking care of your marriage every single day. As I said in Chapter Two, marriages are subject to the laws of physics including the law of entropy which boils down to "things fall apart."

Your marriage will naturally disintegrate if you do not exert a greater energy than entropy to keep it going well. An uncultivated garden does not produce what you want. The good flowers die and weeds take it over almost overnight. Whether we are talking laws of thermodynamics or effective gardening practices, the point is the same. You have to put effort into a relationship just to stay ahead of all that can go wrong. Much of that effort lies in communication.

One darn thing about life is that it is so daily. We are creatures of habit and routine. If we are not very conscious, intentional and purposeful about the habits we form in our present family life we will default each day to the way we were wired by the nature and nurture of our early years. When we marry, we quickly form patterns of communication that may be helpful or hurtful to our relationship. When Jake and Jillian came to see me, I told Jillian that when she is reacting to being disappointed and frustrated by Jake, "little Jillian" is driving the bus of the communication. This is because little Jillian's father was an alcoholic who was no help to the family and her mother was too busy to pay much attention to Jillian. Jillian was programmed by those childhood experiences to take Jake's household slackness as abandonment by the partner she loves and needs. It was an all too familiar feeling.

Finding Jake's shoes in the family room tapped into a reservoir of sorrow in Jillian that was formed by having her needs ignored. Jake would usually say, "Jillian you are overreacting." Little did he know that it was a 10 year old child in the room who was yelling at him about his shoes. You can see why it would have been helpful for him to have known in the beginning of their marriage about her childhood experiences. A more compassionate response would be, "I know it bothers you when I leave my things around the house. You must be tired of picking my stuff up. I will try harder to put things away." Using tender words reaches the heart of a wounded person.

A consciously aware Jillian knows that she brought these vulnerable feelings to their marriage. She must then be intentional to *ask for what she needs* in a way that helps Jake respond to her requests positively rather than always criticizing him for getting it wrong. She is more likely to gain his cooperation if she says, "It actually hurts my feelings when I see you have left your things out for me to pick up. I feel like you are not supporting keeping the house neat and clean. I really appreciate it when you put things away. Please try harder to remember that we both have to keep things in order." Hopefully, Jake would try to keep in mind that doing his part at home is a big part of showing love to Jillian. His expressing gratitude for all she does would also be supportive.

Empathy and compassion come more naturally to some people than others. Again, this is attributable in part to temperament and in part to past life experiences. Tuning in to your mate's feelings is essential to a successful conversation. This is especially challenging when it is not how *you* are feeling in the situation or how *you* think you would feel if you were in your partner's shoes. Please do not argue about feelings. I hear couples say to each other, "You shouldn't feel that way!" You can ask for different behaviors from your mate, but you cannot ask for different feelings. Starting a difficult conversation with a statement of compassion gets things off to a non-threatening start. Jillian might begin her request for help by saying in a gentle tone, "Jake, I know you are tired when you get home from work and it feels good to get out of your work clothes. I am just asking that you put things away as you take them off. I feel so much better when I don't have to pick things up."

* * *

I grew up with an extremely critical parent. When I feel the need to express dissatisfaction to my mate, the words that immediately form in my mind are downright hateful! They are the words I heard as a child. Sometimes I begin a difficult conversation with my partner only to become strangely silent. My partner will say, "Well, aren't you going to finish what you were going to say?" My reply is "I am CENSORING!" That means I'm mentally clicking through possible statements, trying to eliminate all the ineffective, hurtful, and habitual ones I might have said. It often takes a while for me to get to one I believe is okay to say out loud. If people would employ this one technique – censoring, eliminating the use of old **unsuccessful** conversation techniques they have observed, experienced or used - it could save a lot of marriages.

* * *

If you censor your initial inappropriate, ineffective reaction and ask for what you need in a gently instructive way, it will be far more effective than criticizing or nagging your mate. Remember, men particularly hate conversations from which they come away feeling inadequate.

If you are not careful to be conscious and intentional when attempting to communicate, especially to resolve conflict, you will typically wait until you are fed up with something and then attack. You erupt like a volcano. There is a tone and/or volume a person can use in initiating a conversation that immediately puts the other person's hackles up. A harsh beginning signals to your mate "Oh no, here it comes."

John Gottman's research indicates that most conversations end in the same tone they started with. If you want the conversation to end well you better start it well such as with an effort to express empathy. To start out well involves your being careful. Ask yourself "What is it I want to gain from this?" Consider also, "What should I keep in mind about my spouse that will influence a positive response when I bring this up?" Vital to note: Nagging, criticizing and lecturing do not lead to achieving positive goals.

People who study relationship behaviors will tell you that no argument should last more than 3 to 7 minutes. You'll probably get the important ideas on the table in that amount of time. After that you will get off the subject or start repeating yourself while escalating in volume and intensity.

If you plan what you need to say and how to say it, you will be able to keep it short and to the point. Long fights are exhausting and often painful. They leave a couple open to saying things they later regret. Staying in a fight a long time is a sign that one or both of you is trying to "win" which is never helpful to the resolution. In a short argument you may be more able to maintain kindness and a sense of humor and, on that account, you may walk away with a solution.

* * *

In her book, "Hold Me Tight," Dr. Sue Johnson describes a pattern of interaction she calls the Protest Polka. One partner approaches the other partner with a complaint or criticism and the other partner responds with defensiveness and withdrawal. When he or she withdraws it triggers a negative response— a protest—from their mate. That protest usually comes in the form of more complaining and criticism which is met with more defensiveness and withdrawal. This dance often leads to both partners withdrawing from each other with no further attempt to resolve the conflict. The Protest Polka may generate a permanent distance between the two that can lead to divorce. How many couples say, "We drifted apart."? Perhaps what really happened is they withdrew from each other one too many times. It may take counseling to break old destructive habits of avoidance and learn how to give and receive feedback without defensiveness and withdrawal.

* * *

In 12 Step Recovery programs it is recommended to use an acronym as a guide to making choices. The acronym is **HALT**. The letters stand for hungry, angry, lonely and tired. The wisdom is that if you are in one of these states of mind and/or body, you are likely to make a bad decision or say the wrong thing in the wrong tone. Unfortunately, most couples are relegated by their weekly schedules to communicate late in the day when they are hungry, angry, lonely and/ or tired. This means they often handle difficult situations from their automatic response mode rather than their conscious, thoughtful mode. Exercise caution about what time of day you endeavor to initiate what may be a prickly conversation. Try to consider yours and your partner's state of mind and body when you initiate *any* form of conversation. Even the question "How was your day?" will be met with different responses or non-responses according to the person's HALT status.

Please note, I believe that what we refer to as "venting" is overrated. At the end of a difficult day, the best thing a person can do is leave the day behind and let the emotions go.

When people recount distressing events *in detail* to their spouses, they generally relive the negative emotions themselves and cause discomfort to their mate who is listening. The limbic system is the part of your brain that regulates stress responses. It operates based on your perceptions and thoughts. The limbic system doesn't know the difference between your imagination and what is actually happening. I will explain this in detail in Chapter Five. If you vent to your spouse about stressful events by giving a blow by blow account, you are punishing your mind and body all over again by getting all worked up in the telling of it. It is better to give an overall summary of your day's events and say how they made you feel, sort of like a newspaper story. That way you won't make both of you feel worse instead of better. Effective conversation generates support and having fun. Talking about the day without venting is at its best a way to enter into each other's world a little bit so you can feel more bonded.

By hearing about my partner's work through general descriptions, I can enjoy imagining what is going on each day while we are apart. It helps me be compassionate and to send good vibes to my sweetheart.

When you talk to your mate at the end of the day it is rarely to seek advice. You want to feel that your loved one supports you and is on your side. So, partners should only give advice when it is solicited or if they ask permission to give it. Every mate should try to give *supportive* feedback even if it is only to say "bummer" or "awesome!" Most importantly, *undivided* attention, including eye contact, counts as much as the words do.

$$* \quad * \quad *$$

The pause button on the TV remote control can save your marriage. If you do not have a pause button with your DVR box or TIVO, it would be worth getting this feature. I advise you to have a pause button because being fully present to each other is essential to being supportive and enjoyable companions. The pause button gives you an immediate way to stop and focus on your partner when it is important to do so.

Television and/or Facebook watching can be an enemy to marital intimacy. In our media driven culture, marital partners often dive into their media devices as soon as the evening begins and stay engrossed in them until bedtime. Many people complain about having a TV in the bedroom or their partner taking a phone, laptop or IPad into bed with them because these things are distractions to intimacy. My reply is "The only device that belongs in the bedroom is a vibrator!"

All media devices are not all bad all the time. If a couple watches TV together it can be a fun bonding experience. However, women often complain that their husband won't even look up to respond when spoken to if he is glued to the television. Thus, having a remote control with a pause button is the way to solve communication problems when the TV is on. One person says "hit pause", the pause button is hit, the couple makes eye contact, they converse and then return to the show where it was paused. It takes practice to be *willing* to hit pause but it really helps you to stay available to each other.

In our family room this is a big boost to our communication. For one thing, we use the pause button so we can laugh long and hard without missing the next line in a comedy show. We use the pause button to converse about what we just saw or heard. We use it to stop the action and predict whodunit or what will happen next. In these ways we are together watching TV, fully present and bonding in the pleasure of it. We feel all warm inside when we tell our friends that we have watched every single episode of "Survivor" together.

Unfortunately, media devices can often be a major means of abandoning a mate emotionally. Hunter admitted in counseling that he has come to dread being alone with Isabelle because their conversations make him feel bad about himself and angry and defensive with her. Watching TV or staying on the computer is his way of building protective walls to avoid being close to Isabelle. They've had so many negative interactions he has forgotten that being open and intimate with Isabelle used to feel really good. Good enough to marry her. But now, for Hunter, virtual relationships via the media feel safer. They are not fraught with negativity and he can shut down whenever he wants to. Seeing Hunter turn to TV and the internet instead of her makes Isabelle feel lonely and unloved. Their marriage is hanging by a thread. I am teaching them how to foster intimacy with positive communication. I have insisted that Hunter take a break from the internet and to only watch TV with Isabelle. He's having a hard time walking away from the media. I think he might be addicted! Does this sound familiar?

It is noteworthy that unhappy couples begin to forget how wonderful they once felt together. I ask my clients "When was the last time you truly had fun together, especially without the children?" Their mood immediately lightens if they can easily recall a recently shared pleasurable experience. Or the couple slumps in their seats with a sense of defeat because they cannot remember the last time they enjoyed each other's company. It's not the couples who argue a lot who get divorced, it is the couples who lose their pleasure bond who get divorced. Now get out that remote control and watch a movie or a show together, but use the pause button for a quick communication or maybe even for a *long delay* if you know what I mean.

* * *

I have said a lot about communication dos and don'ts in this chapter but I want to conclude by emphasizing that talking is not the same as bonding. Communication is a means to an end. Couples can find their unique ways of talking to each other that promote supporting each other and having fun together. Saying things like " Thank you," "I'm sorry," "What do you need?" and even "Bummer" and "Awesome!" can go a long way to staying emotionally close. It may be awkward at first but it is never too late to try.

CHAPTER 5

Flooding and
Other Dangers

et's expand on three important parts of communication: choosing **what** to say, **how** to say it and **when** to say it. One suggestion is for you to make an effort to be open to *receiving* feedback without being defensive in a conversation even if you initially disagree with what you hear. Another is to back off when there is anger brewing.

Arrogance and defensiveness are two immediately detrimental responses to clear, constructive communication. Arrogance is being close-minded to another's point of view. It conveys an "I am right and you are wrong" attitude. It may even imply that one participant thinks the other is stupid. It lacks compassion and hinders compromise. Being humble, which is being willing to see another point of view from yours, is an effective way to begin to communicate.

Defensiveness is a conversation stopper, too. Usually if a partner has a defensive response to a statement it is followed by a reversal of blame. If Jillian says "Why don't you move your shoes?" Jake may say "Get off my back! You aren't so perfect either. You spend too much money on clothes." Nothing about that interchange invites further meaningful discussion.

If you wake up every single day and make a renewed commitment to being conscious and intentional in your marriage, you will be more likely to approach conversations in the spirit of lovingkindness. You will be more open to translating your complaints and criticisms into non-threatening requests for what you really need or want. You will hear your mate's requests for support and fun with a mind to join in as opposed to dropping out of the conversations. Like the song goes, "Just a spoonful of sugar helps the medicine go down." Take a deep breath and think before you start talking.

Nobody likes to be with someone who goes on and on talking something to death. I find that people who talk a subject into the ground are trying to get the other person to agree with them. It comes across as a brow-beating lecture. Sometimes a partner talks a lot because it is the only way the person knows to be with their mate and get attention. For whatever reason, talking too much will alienate your spouse and make your mate immune to having meaningful conversation when it is needed. This goes for spouses and children.

Men often complain that they really hate to hear minute details about things. They especially hate hearing about the illnesses and other problems of people they barely know. Gentlemen, you need to know that women like to talk about people because they are, for the most part, relationship-oriented creatures. Please try to patiently indulge your wife's need to tell you about Uncle Harry's operation. She may then be more likely to listen to you explain how to solve the world's problems.

Unfortunately, some partners don't have much to talk about besides gossip. If this applies to you, you may want to brush up on your mate's topics of interest. I have learned to be semi-fluent in the languages of NASCAR and golf even though neither is particularly important to me. Can you converse with your spouse about things that interest him or her as well as your own interests?

If your mate is a stay at home parent, he or she is likely starved for adult conversation when you get home. We know you may be tired of interacting through your work day, but please summon the energy to have a conversation with your partner in the evening. I suggest to people who work outside the home that they spend the time driving home from work imagining getting home and interacting with the family and being truly present to them. This mental rehearsal can help you summon that last ounce of energy to do the right thing upon arrival. Even a little bit of well-aimed attention at the end of a day can go a long way towards marital bliss.

* * *

Another guideline for effective communication involves knowing when to call an end to a conversation because it is going nowhere fast or somewhere awful. It is never a good idea to pursue a conversation when one or the other person is flushed with anger or anxiety. In marriage counseling I hold up a picture of a scale of 1 to 10. I explain that this represents one's physiological and psychological state of arousal. When a stimulus causes a person's internal state of agitation to rise to above a 5, there is a diminished brain capacity for reasonable thinking and behavior.

The part of the brain in charge of our response to stress is not a conscious, "thinking" part of the brain. The limbic system is in a more primitive part of the brain. It is command central for monitoring all the automatic functions in our entire internal system such as respiration, digestion, circulation and even eye-blinking. Everything hums along nicely until an alert signal registers. In a caveman's brain, this alert to possible danger was all about survival. It was then and is now about initiating the behavioral responses of fight, flee or freeze. The activating stimulus is the *perception* of danger. In our modern world, danger is most often defined by what an *individual* sees as a threat or as an obstacle to his or her purposes, safety and well-being. These things are rarely actual saber tooth tigers on the prowl, (although we have had some bears in our neighborhood lately.)

This can mean that a ringing phone or a rude co-worker are saber tooth tigers to you because you perceive them as a threat or an obstacle or even just a sudden surprise. You are trying to get to an appointment in a hurry and you hit a traffic jam. You see this as an obstacle to your goal of arriving on time and possibly as a threat to your well-being because you will be in trouble with the boss if you are late. When you perceive the traffic jam as a problem your limbic system responds as if it is a real tiger coming after you. Or at home, your partner's voice suddenly gets a decibel or two louder and your brain experiences this as a threat to the conversation, yourself or your relationship.

The limbic system prepares your body to do what will ensure your survival by "flooding" it. The "flood" consists of hormones and other body chemicals that give you extra energy and physical readiness to respond. This includes adrenaline, cortisol and cholesterol. Most of the blood in your body goes to your muscles for immediate use. This means the prefrontal cortex, the conscious and thinking part of the brain, becomes minimally functional due to the limited blood supply. Even your senses are dulled in processing visual and auditory input. Perhaps this is where the term "blind rage" comes from. Scientists refer to this reaction as your being "hijacked" by your primitive brain.

When a partner perceives his or her mate to be a threat or an obstacle the hijack begins. Note that *perception is reality* as far as the limbic system is concerned. Sexual fantasy is a great example of this. If you close your eyes and imagine the "hottest" scene you can conjure up, your body becomes aroused as if you are really there enjoying a good time. Your conscious thoughts send signals to your limbic system all day long. If you are typically a negative and/or fearful thinker your limbic system activates stress responses much more often than a person who has peaceful, positive thoughts. Being a negative person can have long term harmful effects on your health and on your relationships.

Many couples have such an unhappy history of verbal interactions that just the thought of talking can cause an internal "flood". When the mere thought of having a difficult conversation brings on a strong visceral reaction, you will avoid trying to resolve the conflict. Understanding flooding may help you have the courage to try to express yourself.

* * *

An early warning sign of a flood is in the way your body feels. Your heart rate rises to over 100 and you can tell that the adrenaline energy is beginning to surge. At the **first realization** that you are being hijacked it would be best to ask for a time- out from the conversation. I teach my clients to say "I am flooding" or "I sense that you are flooding", followed by "let's cool off some before trying to finish this discussion." Then you each go away to breathe, take a walk, have a talk with yourself, pray or whatever works to get back below a 5 on the scale of 1 to 10. For some people this may only take 20 minutes or less. However, when you have reached beyond an 8 on the scale it may take up to 2 hours to calm down.

By the way, if you ask your partner for a time-out due to anger when their flood is above a level 7, it will probably make him or her madder. It is really helpful if one or both of you can feel the build-up of tension as it reaches a level 5 so you can *agree* to call off the conversation for a little while. If your mate is already flooded you need to say, "I can't talk about this right now," and quickly exit. He or she may try to follow you to keep arguing. Simply try to go to a room with a door or even get in your car and lock it. Nothing good can come from staying in a very heated conversation because you will eventually lose your cool, too.

As I explained before, the part of your brain that virtually shuts down when you flood, the prefrontal cortex, is where the functions of reasoning and inhibition lie. The prefrontal cortex is the part that thinks "I wouldn't say that if I were you" to the part wanting to call your mate an ugly name or to make a verbal threat. (This "wise brain" also shuts down when you drink too much. That is why being drunk is called being "impaired".) When people argue while flooded they aren't having a productive discussion, they are "throwing harpoons" at each other. The limbic system is in charge and giving a "fight to the death" command. "Staying in the ring" if you are under this influence will probably lead to your fighting until someone is literally or figuratively mortally wounded. A great deal of domestic violence occurs because the people involved continue to pursue an argument while one or both participants are flooding. It is notable that when one person floods everyone in the room eventually floods. This includes your children and your pets.

I used to be the director of a Family Services domestic violence program. Part of the job was interviewing men who had been charged with assault on a female. When appropriate, I would enroll them in our program which we now refer to as anger management. Time and time again I would listen to a man tell his story regarding an assault starting with "she wouldn't get out of my face!" There is never, ever an excuse for assault. Yet, I could see that if one person follows the other person from room to room continuing to engage in an argument, something bad will eventually happen. It usually takes two to agree to a time-out but only one to *escalate* a fight. Knowing when to be quiet is a key to safe and successful conflict resolution.

When my partner and I discuss finances I sometimes have to call time-out several times before we can reach closure. It took a while for my mate to see these time-outs as positive action rather than pure avoidance. Over the years I have become a far better money manager because we patiently worked through these emotional discussions, time-outs and all. A couple's mutual faith that they will actually return to the discussion rather than letting it go unresolved is vital.

* * *

Some couples refuse to "stay in the ring" long enough to reach a conclusion to a difficult discussion even though no one is flooding.

I have met hundreds of people in my practice over the years who tell me they avoid conflict at any cost. Their motto is "I hate confrontation." Some personality types are born with an aversion to rocking the boat because they like peace and quiet and/or they want to please all the people all the time. A majority of folks who hate confrontation came from homes where conflict was not managed well. Some people who just won't "fight" have been victims of violence in previous relationships as children and/or as adults. They need to talk to their mates early in their relationships about their fear or dislike of confrontation or even "heated discussions". It takes patience and understanding to help your conflict-avoidant mate to trust you enough to stay with you in a difficult conversation. You will especially need to employ the guidelines given in this chapter to keep both of you involved in important communication.

In my office, I often observe a couple engaging in arguments, and I make note of their patterns of communication. One phenomenon I see pretty regularly is that of one partner hearing the other express criticism and immediately saying, "You're right, I am a terrible person. I am always wrong. I don't see why you even stay with me." This is usually followed by tears and/or a silent shut-down. Many people are subject to this "all or none" way of looking at feedback. Not many things have to be seen as all good or all bad in order to alter behaviors. People who have had troubled childhoods are especially prone to being "all or nothing" thinkers as adults. It really hinders conflict resolution in marriage. If you tend to flood every time you get honest feedback from your mate, you may need counseling. As prescribed earlier in this chapter, you must somehow learn to breathe deeply and slow down your verbal response until you have thought through what you want to say and/or call a short time-out to talk yourself off the ledge.

Research has found that men in general dislike talking about problems more that women do. A lot of men I have met truly believe they can "never be good enough" to please their wives. In their

minds a discussion is a disguise for bashing. Ladies, men are morti-
fied of feeling like failures! In Dr. Gary Chapman's "The Five Love
Languages," he explains that "words of affirmation" are vital to filling a mate's love tank. If you each have been intentional every day in
providing encouraging words of love and appreciation to each other,
even a conflict-avoidant mate is more likely to be open to resolving
a problem through communication. On the other hand, you can be
sure that if you start a conversation in attack mode your beloved will
run like a scared rabbit or snarl right back at you.

Although some people resist conversation by fleeing or fighting,
many others simply shut down before your very eyes and refuse to
respond in any way. They freeze. Sometimes the freeze is from
fear and many times the freeze is a "stonewall", a stubborn refusal
to engage. This sort of resistance is frustrating and even infuriat-
ing to the person who wants to talk. It creates a terrible negative
feedback loop between the two people. The more she wants to talk,
the more he seems to resist talking. The quieter he is, the angrier
she gets. The angrier she gets, the more he freezes. Dr. Harriet
Lerner explains this "loop" in her books "The Dance of Anger" and
"The Dance of Intimacy." Marriage expert, Dr. Sue Johnson, calls
it the "Protest Polka." Only by being aware of and careful with each
other's feelings can a couple overcome this cycle of avoidance.

In my counseling practice, I encourage couples to reserve difficult discussions for our sessions so I can coach them in forming
effective response modes with each other. As they practice new ways
of communicating, the trust is slowly built and old feelings of fear
and resistance can be replaced with hope. We are building towards
having conversations that lead to supporting each other and having
fun together. I hope the pointers in this chapter will help you do the
same.

CHAPTER 6

Let's Talk About Sex...
Everyone Else Does

Something that sets human beings apart from other animals on the planet is our ability and desire to engage in sex for reasons other than procreation. For other species, sex is part of their rhythm of life, no more and no less. For us humans, sex has been one of our greatest obsessions individually and culturally for centuries.

In 21st century Western culture, sex is power. Sex sells everything from cars to toothpaste. Sex certainly sells magazines, TV shows and movies. Pornography is a multi-billion dollar industry. We refer to "sexy shoes" and "sexy food." Apparently attaching sexiness to *anything* elevates its desirability. You would have to live alone in a cave to avoid being assailed with sexual messages almost every hour of every day. It is probable that selling sex or using sex as a means of selling things is the foundation of our modern economy.

I believe marriages today are undermined by this culture of sex. Children are entering adolescence exposed to sexual messages through every form of media. By the time they reach their 20's most young adults have had multiple sexual partners and have listened to their peers talk about their sexual experiences. This means that they enter marital relationships with comparisons and expectations about sex like no generation before them. Since expectations are resentments waiting to happen, our sex-saturated world has surely produced resentments in the bedrooms of America robbing couples of their conjugal happiness.

Too many couples start their married life wanting their sexual relationship to be "normal." They want to believe the sex they are having is as great as the article in Cosmopolitan magazine says it can be. They count how many times a week they have sex and how many orgasms are achieved in a sexual encounter. Unfortunately, this becomes a pressure that can diminish sexual pleasure and may ultimately hamper performance. We have gone from the former days of "let's get drunk and screw" to the present obsession with enhancing sexual experiences through devices, pills, creams and how-to manuals. Ironically, there has seldom been a time in our history more fraught with sexual buzz-killers, particularly stress and fatigue. We intuitively know that the best sex usually happens when each partner is relaxed and "in the moment" but our lives seldom allow us that luxury. Sadly, the couples I meet in counseling have high hopes regarding the quality and frequency of the sex they think they should be having, but the actual circumstances of their lives are not conducive to having the time, energy or emotional closeness for good sex. The equation in such a marriage— high expectations plus failed delivery—equals sexual misery.

With all that said, it is important to report what was found in numerous research surveys done in the first decade of the 21st century. Between 40 to 50 percent of all married people said they were satisfied with their sex life. The frequency of sex was a contributing factor to the level of satisfaction even more than the frequency of orgasm. Married people have more sex than single people do. Married people have more varied sexual practices than single people do. And some married women surveyed admitted that they sometimes had sex with their partners in order to get them to help around the house. Hey, at least they are having sex! So, we may surmise that marriage can be an excellent context for satisfying sex.

* * *

If marriage is good for sex then what goes wrong? Researchers have found that a major factor in the waning of marital sex is the "de-eroticization" of one's partner. In other words, when your spouse becomes more of a friend or a roommate on a daily basis, you may have a stable marriage but the frequency of sex will drop off. An interesting fact is that men are more often the ones that back away from a regular sex life and it most often happens really early in the marriage, usually in the first five years. Another vulnerable time-frame in marriage that poses a challenge to maintaining a sex life is when the couple's children enter adolescence, probably because the demands of work and family life are at their peak during those years.

Marriage counselors rarely hear that "everything is great" in the sex department when other things are in crisis enough to bring a couple to counseling. Interestingly, sexual dissatisfaction is not usu-ally the presenting problem when a couple comes in unless they are specifically seeking sex therapy. I've learned that if I don't bring it up it won't be mentioned for several sessions. Couples usually say during the intake interview that they want to communicate better. What counselors know is that "communicating better" is a code for "creating intimacy" in all areas of married life.

When two people fall in love and the initial sexual chemical PEA is at its peak, the frequency and intensity of lovemaking seems as natural as breathing. You can't imagine that it will ever be any dif-ferent. Actually, studies have found that two people can't sustain that level of *intense* physical PEA-attraction for more than two years. It's as though the love potion wears off and you see your partner through different eyes. This is when some people may say "I'm not in love with you anymore." In fact, when this compelling attraction begins to wane it is the emotional connection you've created up until then that sustains you. For most couples sex gets better with time even though the chemistry is different. Dopamine and oxytocin are pleasure-related brain chemicals that are sustainable over a lifetime of love with your mate. Sexual intimacy strengthens the emotional bonds in a marriage and helps maintain overall satisfaction with each other until death do you part. I can't emphasize enough that sexual pleasure should be defined by the couple and not by our media culture or by comparison to what is perceived to be what other people are doing.

* * *

Tragically, the absence of sexual contact in a marriage can create a terrible "negative feedback loop" between the partners based on disappointment and resentment. The loss of a satisfying sex life between mates can bring on a cycle of guilt, shame and emotional withdrawal. For many modern couples, the points of origin in the negative cycle are stress and fatigue in one or both partners. A mate may be drained by daily responsibilities at work and at home. Working mothers seem to be the most susceptible to "running on empty" because so much is going out of her emotional tank to the children and adults in her life after a full day in the workplace. By bedtime each night she just wants to collapse and go to sleep.

Meanwhile, her husband craves her attention and wants to relax by having sex. If she says "No, I'm too tired," he feels rejected and frustrated. Furthermore, his need for sexual release builds day after day. He gets grumpy and may be critical towards his wife. When he's not very nice to her she wants even less to do with him sexually. This vicious cycle is the negative feedback loop of desire, initiation, rejection, distancing, more rejection…etc. Sometimes this scenario occurs with the husband being tired and stressed and the wife resenting the lack of sex. No matter who has lost interest and who is filled with resentment, the diminishing of a couple's sexual intimacy usually weakens their overall sense of closeness. However, there are couples who mutually agree that sex is not important to them and they may foster other ways to feel intimately connected.

Craig and Carol were so busy with their careers and preschool children that they could barely find time for a counseling appointment. They each came from a family in which mom and dad were good role models for marriage. Wow, is that rare! Because Craig and Carol know how positive a marriage can be, they realized things were not currently going well. We discussed several aspects of their relationship that needed a tune-up.

When we got to the subject of sex they both sighed and said, "Things were better before we had kids." They admitted that their focus shifted to the children to the exclusion of making time for each other. They had also gotten in the habit of allowing the children to sleep in their bed with them fairly often. Craig reported feeling that he was last on Carol's list for time and affection. Carol said she needed more time for herself to renew her energy. She could not remember the last time she had thought about sex because she felt so drained much of the time. Couples such as Craig and Carol frequently cite the lack of attention to each other and lack of energy as reasons they avoid sex.

Carol and Craig worked together with me to form strategies to bring emotional closeness and sex back to their relationship. When couples fall in love they start out "face-to-face," focusing on each other. When children enter the picture and/or careers are being established, the marriage may become a "side-by-side" endeavor. The couple's energies are no longer directed towards each other's needs and happiness. As with Carol and Craig, the sexual relationship can suffer from this. By planning time each week to connect emotionally there comes a greater openness to sexual intimacy. When this couple became intentionally committed to devoting meaningful time to one another and to helping each other with household duties every week, the sexual negative feedback loop was reversed.

* * *

A wife may feel that her husband regularly "pesters her for sex," typically with unromantic overtures such as grabbing or groping her in the kitchen after supper or making crude remarks. It amazes me how many times I hear that a man will continue these ineffective approaches even after he's been told countless times that this is unwanted by his mate. He is reaching out for sex without first consciously and intentionally building a loving bond between them through non-sexual behaviors.

Not all men can or want to pursue sex when there is an emotional void in the relationship, but many men are ready and able whenever and wherever. On the other hand, almost without exception women report needing "emotional foreplay" in order to be responsive to their husbands' advances. Most women want to be led into lovemaking by actually feeling loved and attended to outside of the bedroom. It is a sure bet that if her tank is empty she will not have the energy or desire to participate in sex. Note to men: If you want more sex, as the old song says, "Try a little tenderness."

Women often tell me they have sex because they feel guilty about their sexually-neglected husband's frustration. This, for some men, is better than nothing. But for other men and women these "I give in, let's get it over with" sexual encounters can become the seed of sexual dysfunction because it increases the likelihood of performance pressure for one or both partners. However, it is noteworthy that women often benefit from giving sex a try even when they are not in the mood when they start out. It is like they have to "warm up the engine" a bit in order to get into it. Also, a lot of women report that a non-orgasmic quickie is fine with them to meet the need for physical intimacy when circumstances are less than ideal for extended lovemaking. In those situations the husband must set aside the goal of having his spouse "fully satisfied" and accept sex as his wife's loving kindness towards him. She is going for an emotional connection rather than an orgasm. It can still be meaningful for both of them without all the fireworks.

* * *

I have often recommended to busy couples that they make time to have sex on the same day every week. Knowing that Thursday night is coming helps to remove the need for one mate asking the other for sex every day thus creating a cycle of guilt and frustration. Scheduling for sex also gives the partners the opportunity to plan the evening more carefully to save energy for lovemaking. The husband and wife may even engage in a bit of fantasy during the day in anticipation of being together that night. When I make this suggestion it is almost always met with skepticism and resistance. "It won't be romantic if it isn't spontaneous!" I reply, "How is being spontaneous working out for you?" If they give it an earnest effort, couples report that to their surprise this idea works out well and can lead to having sex more than once a week.

As opposed to simply being out of sync in the weekly schedule, actual sexual dysfunction may be characterized by an impairment of desire, arousal and/or orgasm. For instance, a man who has been turned down numerous times for sex may experience premature ejaculation when the couple finally gets together. This may create anxiety for him when he approaches his wife in the future fearing that it will happen again. His anxiety affects his ability to have and keep an erection and he feels like a failure again. Subsequently, his thoughts and feelings contribute to the evolution of an actual dysfunction as opposed to having a disappointment once in a while.

A woman may find sex to be painful on enough occasions that she begins to avoid it. Or a wife may feel that her husband wants sex more than he wants *her* and feels angry about that. The anger extinguishes her desire. Sexual dysfunction can take on a life of its own all too quickly when negative emotions interact with performance. The fear of failure or rejection can lead a man or woman to avoid sex with his or her mate to the point that the sexual relationship essentially ends.

* * *

Recent research has shown that having a "good enough" sex life is a dimension of married life that can exist even as other parts of the marriage are strained. Dr. Barry McCarthy found in his studies that addressing marital problems is not hierarchical as in one solution leads to another solution which leads to another in pyramid fashion. Marriage counselors have traditionally seen marriage repair in this way, usually with sexual dysfunction being at the top of the pyramid as the last thing to fix. That meant sexual problems would be addressed after we fixed communication, emotional intimacy and/ or addiction in some chronological order. It isn't that all of these problems should not be addressed, but it is simply more effective to address them simultaneously. Dr. McCarthy believes if one area of a marriage is improving it can aid improvement in other areas at the same time. This may require seeking help from more than one specialist as you work on your marriage. For instance you may go to both a certified sex therapist and a marriage counselor during your course of treatment. Or one of you may go into a recovery program to address addiction while you are in marital therapy. It is usually a good idea to have a medical evaluation to check for hormonal imbalances or vascular impairments and to see if there is a medication side effect to blame for sexual dysfunction. In most cases your insurance will cover these concurrent evaluations and therapies.

* * *

Let me explain a bit more about sex therapy. Certified sex therapists assess the roots of dysfunction and offer help in correcting the problems. A skilled sex therapist will take a sexual history in individual sessions with each partner. This will uncover sexual secrets, traumas and behaviors that influence the current sexual dysfunctions. A sexual treatment plan is then mapped out with the couple and homework assignments are given. Sex therapy is a process that requires patience, persistence and hope. Fortunately, many couples have utilized therapy to restore a satisfying sex life to their marriage. It would be a tragic mistake to remain in denial about the lack of sex for so long that one or the other of you seeks sex outside of marriage or goes deep into the world of pornography and internet sex.

The most important aspect of improving your sex life is *finding what is right for the two of you.* This is not gauged by a survey in Glamour magazine or locker room discussions of sexual conquests. It is measured by the pleasure and closeness it brings to your relationship on a regular basis. The solutions may or may not include intercourse or consistent experiences of orgasm. The message here is don't give up on sex! Just change your expectations and behaviors to accommodate every stage and season of your life together and keep a sense of fun in the bedroom. Nothing else matters but the two of you and your mutual satisfaction.

CHAPTER 7

Scraggy Toenails and Hairy Legs

"I wish he'd look at me the way he just looked at her," Carrie thought as she and her husband, Kyle, claimed their chairs by the neighborhood pool. She settled into the lounger as she glanced at Kyle beside her. She began to evaluate how things had been with them lately. Kyle had approached her for sex earlier in the week and she half-heartedly participated although he hadn't showered and his late day stubble was rough. She noticed his toenails were long, sharp and, frankly, gross. Over the past several months his method of seduction had been reduced to grabbing her breast and saying "Wanna go for it?" He always aimed for her satisfaction and usually succeeded, but it felt like just sex, not lovemaking. Carrie sighed and went to sit on the edge of the pool.

That evening Kyle considered initiating sex with Carrie. He made note at the pool that she had shaved her legs. He asked for sex nearly every day even though he knew Carrie would only go along with it once or twice a month. "I have to play the odds to get the pay-off," he reasoned. Memories of the good old days when they had sex several times a week were growing dim. Now, Carrie wears lounge pants and a tee shirt to bed every night and complains of how exhausted she is.

Kyle looked up at Carrie when she sat down on the edge of their bed. "She seems like she's in a good mood right now," he thought. He reached for her breast. "Wanna go for it?"

Carrie and Kyle are a couple whose physical pleasure bond is dwindling week to week, month to month. Sadly, this marriage is not that unusual in 21st century America. For hundreds of thousands of couples romance has crashed like the '08 stock market and never rallied. How can this happen in such a sexually oriented culture?

Over the years as a counselor I have asked men and women to list the "buzz killers" in their marriages. What was or was not happening in their relationship or their home that diminished their sexual desire for each other, often in the prime of their physical lives? There are several things that make the list time and time again. Most of these won't surprise you, but when it comes to your own relationship you may not have given these items much thought. As I share with you the ideas I gained from listening to people about what the buzz killers are for them, I hope you will see how the little things can add up, and how easily you may lose sight of the behaviors that were once so obviously important to maintaining sexual attraction. When you quit being conscious and intentional about maintaining your sexual bond it can slip away never to return.

* * *

Imagine your home as a greenhouse in which you plant, nurture and protect all aspects of your marital relationship. Romance will thrive in your marriage if you keep the environment (the physical setting) and the atmosphere (the climate) in your greenhouse in top shape. It does not matter whether you live in a mansion or a hut, how you live inside is what counts.

Let's start with your *environment*. It may be a stretch for you to see the link between romance and how tidy your house is, but many husbands and wives say that dirt and clutter in their home, especially in the bedroom, make them not want to be in it at all much less to enjoy physical intimacy there. One male client told me that unclean sheets and clothes strewn all over the bedroom made him want to sleep on the sofa. Believe me, there is a link between lack of sexual desire and overflowing trash, dishes in the sink and piles of dirty laundry. A female client announced in a session, "Clean laundry equals love!" This lady felt most receptive to her husband when he actively participated in doing household chores and the house felt orderly. Pack rats and couch potatoes along with other kinds of poor housekeepers can bring their greenhouses to ruin. Thankfully, mutual efforts to maintain a great environment in a home can boost a couple's love life.

Remember that if you are protecting the sexual intimacy in your marriage you must have a "sacred place." Couples need an emotional and physical oasis as a retreat from all other things. Decorating your bedroom to be comfortable and pleasant is a vital part of making it a sanctuary for sexual love. Nice clean sheets, soft lighting, cool temperature and peaceful quiet can put you in the mood for love. I cannot emphasize enough how important it is to keep pets and children out of your bed nearly all of the time. If they join you it is by invitation only. That's what kennels, door locks and baby monitors are for!

∗ ∗ ∗

More than one mate has complained that bad bedroom habits can detract from romance. Things like eating in bed, using the smartphone or a laptop in bed and having the TV on in the room are cited as buzz killers. If your mate complains that you snore, please do all you know to do to minimize the problem. If your partner does not want to sleep with you because of snoring, it may make it harder to get together for sex. If sleeping in the same bed is not possible for whatever reason, you both must be especially conscious and intentional about "rendezvous" efforts.

It seems that now more than ever couples don't sync their bedtimes with each other. Shiftwork is one reason for this, but often it is simply due to personal preferences and "body clock" differences. Being on the internet, especially looking at email or Facebook, is frequently cited as a reason for separate sleep schedules. Ironically, the epidemic of internet pornography addiction flourishes when mates surf the net while their partners sleep. Folks, please enter the sacred place *together*. Rediscover the sweetness of pillow talk and falling asleep with your arms around each other or your hands touching.

* * *

Maintaining your marital "greenhouse" not only includes the physical environment but also requires the control of the internal *climate*, the atmosphere. For human beings the greenhouse climate depends on the moods and behaviors of the people who live in it. When a couple agrees that they have had a nice day together, it usually means it has been a day free of conflict and full of pleasant companionship. As I have previously mentioned, in "The Five Love Languages," Gary Chapman proposes that acts of service, words of affirmation, quality time together, gifts and touch are means of conveying and cultivating love in a marriage. Just think about how great the atmosphere in your home would be if the two of you were conscious and intentional in your efforts to be thoughtful, helpful, affirming and attentive to each other physically and emotionally. Intimacy would be naturally flourishing in such a greenhouse.

* * *

Some of my clients complain that major emotional buzz killers for them are spousal grumpiness and/or outright hatefulness. It is hard to make love to a porcupine. No one wants to be close to a spouse who criticizes, nags and complains. Wives have often lamented in our counseling sessions, "I can't understand how my husband can be angry and mean in the living room and immediately want sex in the bedroom. I can't turn my feelings on and off like that." Or husbands have said, "She treats me like a child. She tells me what to do and is never satisfied with how I do it. It is hard to see her in a romantic way." Generally, negativity is a real turn off to tender feelings of affection. Just talking about negative things related to the children, work, politics or the neighbors can harm the atmosphere. Simply being pleasant and positive goes a long way in keeping romantic love alive.

Sexual love does not grow well in a greenhouse that is too cold. You won't have a cozy evening with a mate who has been isolated, disinterested and unaffectionate all day. Some homes are "cold" because one or both partners are seldom there to keep it warm. There has to be careful attention paid to how much time is spent with your family vs. being at work, playing sports and socializing with people without your spouse. Even good things like church work and other volunteer projects can take you away from your loved ones so much that things grow cold at home.

Joseph and Nola affirm that they love each other and want to have a happy, satisfying marriage. When they came to me for help, they agreed that they felt a growing distance between them. I learned that both of them were very busy with things away from home. Nola called herself a "golf widow". She explained that Joseph is an avid golfer who insists on playing 9-18 holes once or twice every weekend. Joseph says this is the way he relaxes from his work week and spends time with his friends. He described Nola as overcommitted to volunteering at church and the kids' school. "Every time the church door opens she falls in," Joseph complained. Nola admitted she has a hard time saying no to requests for help. As you can imagine, their greenhouse was not very warm and their relationship sorely needed tending. We focused on strategies for each of them to enjoy their activities away from home while being more balanced in the amount of time they devoted to them.

They both gave up some of what they liked to do in order to gain meaningful hours together, growing love.

* * *

Fostering romance in your marriage includes what I call "emotional foreplay" which needs to happen throughout the day and all over the house, not just at night in the bedroom. Emotional foreplay is defined by what is meaningful *to your partner* as a lead up to sex. I brought up in Chapter Six that women often complain to me about their husbands grabbing and groping them as a "come on" for intimacy. They tell me their husbands persist in doing it even after they have repeatedly asked them not to. Men, the best "come on" is one that is truly *emotionally* appealing. Listen to your wife when she tells you what gets her in the mood for love. It takes thoughtful, sensitive effort to achieve a loving atmosphere everywhere in your home as many hours of the day as possible.

One wife declared to her husband, "Neutral is not the same as nice." Just because you aren't fighting doesn't mean love is being tended to in the greenhouse. Never stop looking for ways to positively impact the temperature in your life together. If you want romance in your marriage, keep the thermostat adjusted. Mort Fertel expands on the details of how to cultivate intimacy in marriage in his book, "Marriage Fitness." It is one of the best how-to books I have ever read because the steps are clearly laid out without a lot of psychological jargon.

In any greenhouse the most beautiful plants have been properly groomed. They need to be trimmed, sprayed and displayed in the best light. In nature, it is the splendid flower that attracts the pollinator. My clients have informed me that the number one physical buzz killer in a relationship is poor personal hygiene and grooming. Both genders report they are not attracted to a body that is not well kept. We aren't necessarily talking about whether a spouse has gained weight or lost hair. It is about smelling fresh and clean. It is about brushed teeth, shaved legs and trimmed toenails. This personal appearance stuff also extends to a mate's manners regarding burping, passing gas, nose picking and butt scratching.

I highly recommend that when you and your mate enter your sacred place together you first engage in at least the most basic "purification rituals," i.e. washing faces, brushing teeth and cleansing the erogenous zones. Bonuses could be a hint of cologne or provocative attire. Animals, even insects, rely on mating rituals for the survival of their species. If you want to have a great sex life with your partner, don't stop the mating rituals after you get married or when you have your first child.

Back to the poolside couple, Kyle and Carrie. They are much too young and vibrant to consider lovemaking as a thing of the distant past. To maintain romance in their marriage the courtship must never end. They are the co-keepers of the greenhouse where their love can thrive. Let's hope that with a good environment and atmosphere in their home they both will always "wanna go for it."

CHAPTER 8

The Huddle

"If Mama ain't happy, ain't nobody happy." Truly, most mothers in American family culture are the hub of the wheel of family life. In counseling with women, I have perceived their great ambivalence regarding the role of "controller." They complain that they are drained of every ounce of their energy by giving so much, but they aren't sure they trust their husbands to pull some weight and "do it right." Many times when I've asked a husband why he doesn't pitch in with household chores and responsibilities he says, "I can't do it to suit her!" His wife will reply, "It's just easier to do it myself." Poor guy. His wife is *saying* one thing, "I'll do it myself," and *feeling* another, "I resent you for leaving it all to me." That husband feels like he cannot win. He may want to make Mama happy but there is no simple route to follow to get her there. What he receives instead is resentment.

Resentment unwittingly begins with someone's unfulfilled expectation, hope or dream. Memorize this now, if you didn't in the two earlier chapters where it appeared: "Expectations are resentments waiting to happen." Without a doubt, resentment is the most malignant, destructive force affecting family life today. When resentment becomes bitterness, a marriage is doomed. What I present as a solution to resentment between marital partners is the single most effective tool I offer to couples in counseling. This solution is called The Huddle.

Unfortunately, most expectations in a marriage are not met because they aren't explicitly expressed. Many unhappy women have said, "If he loved me he would know what I need." Or some wives will say, "All he has to do is look around and he could see what needs to be done." In fact, depending on either gender's personality type, he or she may seldom pay attention to details or be disturbed by clutter and disorder. These people usually marry a "neat freak" and discord is therefore built into the relationship. Another scenario is when one mate is a perfectionist and the other just does enough to get by. These are examples of how partners can let each other down. In your marriage, the only hope of pleasing your partner is if clear requests are made by each of you, preferably in the form of a detailed list including a time frame for getting things done. The lists are best presented as a *discussion* rather than a dictation.

Many wives have told me that it seems like their husbands are only distant observers of the day to day maintenance of family life. "He doesn't know the children's schedules or even their teachers' names. He doesn't know how to load the dishwasher or fold laundry. He believes if he mows the lawn he's done his part," laments an unhappy wife. If you look at a family as a sports team you could say that a lot of husbands "don't have their head in the game." This is especially troublesome if both partners in a marriage work full time outside of the home. Surveys of American couples consistently reveal that, of the prevailing problems experienced in marriage, the division of household labor is in the top three.

Too many wives complain that, due to the lack of their husband's participation in household upkeep, they actually work two full-time jobs. "I work all day at the office. Then I come home and my other job begins. I collapse into bed each night exhausted. I get up a few hours later and start all over again while my husband sleeps an extra hour," cries a harried wife and mother. Granted, sometimes it is the husband who carries the main responsibility for keeping the family going, but most often it falls to the wife.

For a dual career couple, the responsibility for maintaining the home life should be equally shared. Perhaps unknowingly when a man says, "I try to *help* my wife at home," he implies that he thinks the job is mainly hers and his is to *help*. If his wife is expecting him to participate equally in the work at home but there is no plan in place for that to happen, then her expectations are not met and resentment is born. Resentment, that ugly monster, can stomp a family to pieces!

* * *

Let's go back to the analogy of family life as a sports game such as football and your family as a team. The family team is led by you and your spouse as co-captains who devise and guide the execution of the game plan. In a real football game these plays are called during the team huddle. Without a huddle the players have no exact directions for effectively moving towards the goal line. There would be no common vision and not much cooperation in the game. A team without huddles is destined to lose. A family without huddles is destined for resentments.

When I have been able to help a couple establish the *consistent* use of Huddles, they say it changed their family life for the better more than anything else they have ever tried. The Huddle is the husband and wife's best vehicle for making expectations known. You will see that Huddling establishes a higher level of over-all communication than you thought possible. It is the cornerstone of a conscious, intentional and purposeful relationship because it is the ultimate way to *plan* to be supportive and helpful. One wife whose husband now joins her in weekly Huddles proclaimed, "It finally feels like his head *is* in the game." Discussing and planning family life in regular Huddles will help you and your mate feel much more deeply connected. Neither of you will feel like you are "in it alone."

* * *

Here's how I recommend doing a Huddle. You and your partner must establish at least two times a week to meet at a table with a calendar, pencil and notepad. Some families incorporate a spot in the kitchen with a chalk or white board for keeping Huddle information accessible to all family members all the time. Each meeting is meant to be a discussion, not just one spouse dictating to the other. The first weekly meeting is best held on Sunday. The Sunday Huddle is for planning the week ahead. It is the time to remind each other of yours and the children's' activities such as doctor appointments, music lessons and ball practices. You will determine who will chauffeur whom on what days at what times. Also regarding the children, there should be reminders of known tests and projects due at school and/or upcoming teacher conferences or special performances. Keeping track of all these activities requires the precision of a Rolex watch. It is not for the faint-hearted.

The Sunday Huddle is a time to share with each other your respective work, civic, religious, sports and social activities. It helps you anticipate who is available to "carry the ball." The Sunday Huddle should lead to decisions about who will cook supper or help with the children's homework on any given weeknight. It is the opportunity for expectations to be clearly conveyed and for details to be nailed down. Maybe you can even find a way to allow each other a little free time.

Many American families spend thousands of dollars a year eating out or bringing fast food home. Usually, these families don't eat home-cooked food because of the lack of meal planning. If you have done a good Sunday Huddle, it will be on the calendar to lay out the meat to thaw or to start the crockpot in the morning. Most of us have phone apps that can be set to remind us to do things like turn on the crockpot. At our house, we plan the menus for the week and then go shopping after the Huddle to get what is needed for the week's meals. There are couples who actually pull out recipes to browse for fresh ideas as part of the Sunday Huddle. Imagine that!

* * *

In my office, Matthew and Jen brought up an important issue that prompted me to teach them to Huddle. They had been married 12 years and had come to counseling because they knew that being angry at each other much of the time was a terrible way to live. We had established that the anger could be broken down to Jen's resenting Matthew's lack of participation in household duties and to Matthew's feeling defensive about Jen's criticism of him. Jen reported that Matthew came home from work and promptly "tuned out" for the rest of the evening. Matthew said Jen began nagging him the minute he walked in the door. Using the sports analogy, she expected him to jump in and put on his game jersey. He expected to relax and sit on the bench. This was a dysfunctional team. Resentments ate at their marriage.

Jen's deepest resentments stemmed from how difficult she found the hours from 5pm to 7pm on weekdays to be. These were the hours when everyone was tired and hungry. Remember **HALT** from the chapter on flooding? The children would argue with each other instead of doing their homework at the kitchen table. Jen tried to monitor them *and* cook supper, but it was a strain to get it all done especially because she was tired and hungry, too.

In a counseling session, Jen asked if the Sunday Huddle could solicit Matthew's commitment to a plan for coming home from work by 5:30 and taking the homework duty while she cooked, or vice versa. Matthew agreed to her request. In subsequent counseling sessions they both agreed that Huddling about the coverage of those crucial hours greatly reduced tension between them. Their sons seemed calmer, too.

✳ ✳ ✳

The equally vital Huddle each week is the "weekend Huddle" which actually occurs no later than Thursday. This Huddle mainly serves the purpose of preventing "The Sunday Evening Blues." The SEB's are identified by the refrain, "another weekend wasted." How many times have you gone to bed at the end of a weekend feeling disappointed and maybe a bit mad that you didn't do the things you meant to do? The time always seems to get away from you. You have aimlessly wandered through the weekend with vague ideas of what could or should be done, but never quite got it all together. I guarantee that a weekend Huddle will have you singing Hallelujah instead of the blues on Sunday nights.

Because we so often marry our opposite temperament, couples usually have one person who wants to relax and play all weekend and the other has a list a mile long of tasks to accomplish. The weekend Huddle helps you meet in the middle. A well spent family weekend will give everyone a bit of what they want. The weekend Huddle is for explicitly stating your expectations concerning work and play and *specifically* developing a plan. Many of us have hopes and dreams for our weekends that go a whole year without being fulfilled. A good Huddle is where you begin to make a dream come true.

The weekend Huddle begins with the question, "What is your number one priority for this weekend?" There are no right or wrong answers to this question. Matthew may want to watch NASCAR which can take a few hours. Jen may want to get a bedroom closet organized and a squeaky door oiled. They agree to work together on her projects from 9am to noon on Saturday and leave time for him to watch the race, too. With planning, there can be time set aside for a family activity at the park or a cookout with neighbors. What a nice weekend.

It is important to be *specific* about days and times for your activities using your best estimates of how long each thing will take to finish. When couples have come back to sessions with me feeling less than enthusiastic about the results of attempting to Huddle, I ask them to do one while I observe. Without fail, the problem lies in their not being detailed enough. Break the weekend down into blocks of time and plan all of it, even if the plan is to do nothing. Double check that each of you knows what he or she is responsible for.

It is advisable to also discuss the budget for what you want to do. Consider the weather forecast when outdoor plans are being made. Do the kids have ballgames or sleep overs on their schedule? Involving the children in at least part of the weekend Huddle is the very best of team efforts. Couples have reported that their children have enjoyed being included in Huddles. Kids don't want to sit there for the whole time, but they like having an opportunity for input.

"Can't we leave an afternoon unplanned?" asked Matthew. He just might want to go to Home Depot or take a nap. "Let's make love Sunday morning," is Jen's request. Put it all out there. Brainstorm. Write down the plan. Every minute does not have to be filled with activity but without the weekend Huddle the team will almost surely fumble the ball.

$$* \quad * \quad *$$

What to do about "to do" lists? Be realistic regarding how long a task may take. Don't make a list for one day's work so long that you feel overwhelmed from the start. That can lead to saying, "Screw it all," and sitting on the sofa all weekend. Keep in mind you may have an emotional preference for a particular thing to get done sooner rather than later. Go first to the things that bother you the most and enjoy the relief when they are finally done. Assign some of the tasks on your list to the children. It'll build their character.

A Huddle is not meant to be a gripe and complaint session. Huddles can be great for problem solving but no one will want to participate if they anticipate being nagged and criticized. I also recommend that Huddles not be times for venting about your workplace woes and conflicts. I mentioned in a previous chapter that this can bring the mood way down. Conversely, a Huddle is a fine time to celebrate what's been good about a day or a week. I call this "giving a praise report," and it is something to look forward to.

In working with couples about using the Huddle, I've learned that we must agree in a counseling session which of them is in charge of "calling the Huddle." In almost every case the husband asks the wife to call it. It seems that men believe their wives naturally keep a better handle on the major family operations than they do. If this is true in your family it does not mean the man in the family can abdicate all leadership. I am an advocate for husbands and fathers being major contributors to the emotional energy in their families but, as I said in the beginning of this chapter, husbands feel unsure about their roles in the lives of their families partly because of mixed messages from their wives.

Some religious traditions teach that the husband is the "head" of his wife and family. Lots of folks take this to mean that he is the boss, the unquestioned authority. It has been sometimes used to subjugate women. However, the ancient meaning of the word "head" is "source", such as the source of a river. Therefore, the meaning would imply that the *husband* is the point of origin in what I call "the circle of love." The outpouring of love *begins* with him and it flows back to him from a grateful family.

What if men saw it as their role to fill their wives love tanks by intentionally doing the things they know are helpful? What if they believed they were meant to be the ones to *take the initiative* to show love most of the time? I am not talking about initiating sex. I am talking about being the source of the river of love flowing to their wives and families. The good news is that love in marriage flows in a circle when it's flowing smoothly. When a husband complains about his wife never wanting to have sex, the problem may be that she is feeling emotionally and physically drained by all of the demands of family life. Sometimes it is because she is so full of resentment that nothing can circle back in his direction. Whether it is an empty tank or a resentment-clogged tank impeding the flow of love, her husband usually has it in his power to make things better through the "circle of love" concept.

It is a fact that a woman tends to give her emotional energy to the children before she gives to her husband. Often she will give her energy to work, friends, neighbors and the family pets before she gives it to her husband. Here's where the circle of love comes in. A wise husband will make sure he tends to his wife's emotional tank in every way he can because then there will be something in it to return to him. A thoughtful wife will reserve some energy for her husband so he will feel rewarded for keeping her tank full. As always, this circle of love is conscious, intentional and purposeful on the part of both mates and the Huddle helps *plan* for the filling of love tanks. Both Huddles each week should always include providing for you and your mate to have quality time alone together.

An interesting point pertinent to our discussion of the Huddle and the filling of each other's love tanks comes from Mort Fertel's book, "Marriage Fitness." Fertel reminds us it is when we *give* love to our mate that we feel closest to him or her rather than when they give to us. Love flowing out of us makes us feel connected to the recipient and feeling connected is everything in marital bliss.

Couples who incorporate the Huddle in their week have reported that they have improved their overall communication. They say they learned to Huddle about things all week long and feel much more in touch with each other emotionally. Good communication is like sex. The less you have the less you have and the more you have the more you have.

It has been my observation that some couples enthusiastically embrace the idea of The Huddle for only a few weeks. Then they sheepishly admit they've begun to let the Huddle fall by the wayside before it could become a solid habit. Almost without exception, these folks say that the improvements in their marriage stopped going as well when they stopped Huddling. Even when one of you is designated the "Huddle caller" it takes *both* of you to keep the weekly commitment to it. Remember that the sustained effort to meet up will make the Huddle a habit and a habit can become a tradition. Wouldn't it be great to see your children and your children's children keeping The Huddle going!

CHAPTER 9

The Elephant in the Living Room

After nearly forty years of being a marriage and family counselor, I look at houses as I drive by and think "there's a story there." I actually know some of the families who live in those houses either socially or as my clients. If you met one of those families at church, PTA or the neighborhood pool you would see them as a happy family. You might even envy them as the "perfect family." Indeed, a family portrait hangs in the hall of their home, a picture of smiles and apparent harmony. Pretty people having a pretty life. No one on the outside would see that this family is as shattered as the portrait would be if it had crashed on the floor into jagged pieces. That is why in the 12-Step recovery programs it is often said "Don't compare your insides to my outsides."

We live in a world of people most of whom put up a good front. They maintain an image that does not give any hint of internal pain and struggle. Pastors, doctors, lawyers, teachers, business associates and moms in the pickup line at school can be living a "double life." They may be respected, admired and loved in their relationships outside their home and yet with family they are creating heartache and misery. No one but the family ever knows the truth.

Leo Tolstoy wrote "Every unhappy family is unhappy in its own way." Families for which addiction is a factor suffer most often in secrecy. Because members of the family are subject to the rules "don't talk, don't think, don't feel," they usually endure their pain in silence. Addiction is commonly referred to as a "family disease" because the dysfunction affects everyone in the home every day. If a parent or a spouse is an addict, each family member plays a role in reaction to the behaviors and consequences of addiction. This is true even if the relative isn't living there anymore.

It didn't take long for the founders of Alcoholics Anonymous to realize that an adjunct group was needed for the alcoholics' loved ones. Thus, Al-Anon was formed to help address the codependency, anger and heartache experienced by people who live with and/or care about addicts. If you are enduring this pain, it would be worth your time and effort to visit an Al-Anon or Nar-Anon group. You may find emotional support, shared wisdom and experiences, and helpful literature in a local church or civic center meeting room. Almost every town in America has 12-Step recovery groups such as AA and Al-Anon. You may need to visit more than one group to find the one that feels right for you. And then, as they say, "keep coming back."

It is truly amazing how those of us who are adult children of alcoholics or drug addicts are drawn to marry someone who is or will become one. It is that "invisible connection" I referred to in Chapter One. In that chapter I explained that an unconscious part of us wants to fight those childhood battles again but this time, *win*. Sad to say, most often those marital battles open all our old reservoirs of pain and we do what we did growing up in order to survive. I've met many men and women who marry one alcoholic after another even to the third and fourth marriages. There is a saying in AA, "When you do what you always did, you get what you always got." Suffering in silence and repeating behaviors that failed are the first things you want to quit doing.

If you decide to seek professional help, start with looking for someone who is qualified to counsel in the field of addiction. Many people start with their family physician. I have noted that many physicians are as prone to denial as the family is and underestimate the need for a referral to other professionals. A limited number of counselors are trained in addiction treatment, so check credentials. An even smaller number of professionals conduct interventions like you've seen on TV, but you could probably find one in your state who would be available to help you get your loved one to treatment. Most treatment centers can provide guidance in getting help. Don't get discouraged in your search for services.

* * *

Let me briefly explain what an intervention is. In the broadest sense, an intervention is an effort to inspire an addict to seek treatment. Most interventions are joint efforts between family members and professionals to coax a reluctant loved one to enter a specific treatment program at a specific time and place. I have led interventions for three decades. With rare exception, we have succeeded in getting the loved ones the help they needed. I think success is predicated on careful planning and rehearsal with the friends and family in preparation for the actual intervention event. Prior to the intervention we decide what we will be asking the addict to agree to and how it can work for him or her without negative consequences. We have already researched things like their company's policy regarding leave for treatment, insurance coverage and even who will feed the dog if they go to stay a while at a facility. An intervention is a way of creating a crisis for the addict in which he or she is made aware that the family is no longer willing to live in quiet misery and changes must be made. My experience has always been that the interventions are filled with love and support for the addict even while their need for help is being presented. I believe interventions can save families and the lives of addicts.

*   *   *

Not all substance abusers are addicts. Many addiction specialists believe every brain has a 'tipping point" at which it may become an "addicted brain." At that point, the brain cells and neural pathways have functionally changed in their responses to the ingestion of a substance. Addiction occurs when powerful associations are formed in the brain between the release of dopamine and the use of the substance. Dopamine is a chemical in the brain that is strongly linked to pleasure. An addicted brain has a different "relationship" with a substance than a non-addicted brain may have because even thinking about using the substance makes the brain "light up." Many factors are involved as to when the "tipping point" occurs for an individual. These include genetic predisposition, gender, age of onset of heavy use and the amount and frequency of current use. Binging is a form of abuse that often begins in adolescence and creates the risk for the binger to become an addict later in life. Binging may continue to be the way an addict consumes drugs and/or alcohol in a week or a month. Just because an addict does not get drunk or high every day does not mean there is no addiction.

Maia Szalavitz recently published a book questioning the widely accepted theories regarding the origins and treatments of addiction. "The Unbroken Brain" distills 25 years of science and research to pose a theory of addiction as a learning disorder rather than a brain disease. She suggests that there is a broad spectrum of addiction, not just an either-or phenomenon. Because many people are not comfortable with or necessarily helped by using 12-Step programs, it is wonderful there is an ever-evolving variation of approaches to recovery. It is important to explore with counselors and/or treatment centers the philosophy and methods of treatment they currently employ before you have your loved one seek help from them.

You have probably heard the term "functional alcoholic". Millions of alcoholics/substance abusers go to work most days and carry on in life with a good measure of success. I have met many people who think of the homeless people on the street corners as the only alcoholics in their community. In fact they may be your child's school teacher, your family physician or the mom who starts with a glass of wine while cooking supper and has finished the bottle by 9:00. Did you know that over 32 million Americans struggled with a serious alcohol problem in the year 2015?

* * *

Because of the way our brain adapts to substance use, it becomes "rewired" to perceive the substance as necessary for survival. That's how craving is developed. An addicted brain sends *very compelling* messages to the user to "hit me again" with the substance even when the results of getting hit again are themselves increasingly punitive, painful and unpleasant. For many addicts morality becomes mean-ingless when the brain cries for the substance. I had a client come to my office in tears reporting that his crack addict wife had sold their children's toys for drug money.

The later stages of addiction include physical dependency on the substance at which point addicts will experience withdrawal symptoms if they stop using. Withdrawal from drugs or alcohol is at best unpleasant and at worst fatal. Not everyone needs 28 days in a residential treatment center to get sober, but physically dependent addicts do need medical supervision to safely get off a substance. Insurance will cover this stage of treatment under most circum-stances whether in a local hospital or a specialized recovery center.

Families of addicts usually describe them as having a "split personality." There is the sober person who goes to work every day and to the kids' soccer game on Saturday mornings. Then there is the one who is drunk or high and is awful to be around. Once in a while I hear of addicts who are nicer when they are impaired than when they are sober. More often I hear of addicts who are difficult to be around no matter if they are using or are sober. Loved ones describe evenings with a substance abuser as a time of losing the person as he/she becomes increasingly impaired. Their speech changes, their personality changes and their "presence" changes. It feels like abandonment to the family.

From the earliest stages of substance abuse, the abuser is either thinking of getting high, is high, or is coming down from being high. This cycle of use seems to consume the very souls of the addict and their loved ones. I have listened to spouses or children of addicts lament, "Why doesn't he love me enough to stop?" Or "What can I do to get her to give it up?" Self-blame is a common trait of someone who lives with addiction. This is usually fostered by the addicts who are trying to deflect guilt and find excuses for their behaviors.

$$* \quad * \quad *$$

What does it mean that "addiction is a family disease"? There comes a time in the life of the family of a substance abuser at which the loved ones develop a pathology known as "codependency." Codependency has been a term tossed around nebulously to mean "closely attached." In the clinical definition of the term, codependency is characterized by one's obsession with fixing, changing or controlling another person's behavior. If an addict is addicted to a substance, a codependent is addicted to control. It is a vicious cycle of interactions involving manipulation, guilt and often anger.

Family members adopt roles in interacting with an addict that play out for as long as they live with the addict and usually into the rest of their lives. Mothers or fathers may instruct their children to behave themselves so the addict won't use. A child may try to keep everyone amused or another may strive to be perfect so attention will be diverted from the family pain. Although manifested in various ways, family members take responsibility for keeping the family out of harm's way. Adult children of addicts are often over-achievers who feel guilty almost all the time for no apparent reason and they find ways to be caretakers. Or sometimes they have a perpetual sense of hopelessness and may self-sabotage any vestige of personal happiness. As I said before, they also may marry an addict.

* * *

You can gauge whether or not you are codependent by how much time you spend each day thinking about the loved one who abuses substances. The thoughts can be fearful, angry and/or controlling. The thoughts are actually the opposite of self-care thoughts because they are focused on the other person. There is a joke that goes, "What happens to a codependent when she's drowning? Someone else's life passes before her eyes."

Another mark of codependency is difficulty with setting limits and boundaries. Instead, there is a lot of pleading, nagging and threatening without any real consequences. Actually, what family members do is make it easier for the substance abuser to keep making bad decisions by "covering" for them in multiple ways. This is called enabling. Wives of alcoholics will call the spouse's workplace to make an excuse for an absence. A husband may go looking for his wife in a bar so she won't drive drunk. A son or daughter may pour out the parent's alcohol and beg him not to buy any more while loaning him money to go to the grocery store. It is interesting how loved ones will balance the life of the family around the addict's cycles of use. Spouses and children find a way to make it day by day, month by month and year by year. It is this adaptability to dysfunction that facilitates the problems being kept a secret. The best book to read as a resource for overcoming codependency is Melody Beattie's classic "Codependent No More."

When I was a little girl I had a neighborhood friend for several years whose home I never once entered. Most of us were in and out of each other's houses as if we lived there. But this particular friend would make excuses like, "My mom doesn't want the white carpet to get dirty." I'm not sure that in all those years I actually ever saw her mother. She died young as many alcoholics do. Only then was I apprised of what my friend had endured. Almost every year at least one of my clients dies of addiction. I see the anguish and often ambivalent feelings of the loved ones left behind. The guilt and shame can reach beyond the grave.

$$* \quad * \quad *$$

When couples come to me for marriage counseling I assess their respective use of substances, including prescription drugs which are widely abused in our society. If I learn that one or both has a substance abuse problem I tell them we cannot proceed with marital counseling without also seeking help for the substance abuse. Recent studies have shown that counselors do not have to address only one issue at a time. The most effective treatment plan includes simultaneous efforts to improve marital skills *and* to end the abuse of drugs or alcohol, especially since in many cases the substance abuser damages the relationship by becoming very surly or even violent while impaired.

Pearl and Buddy were in my office because Pearl told Buddy if he didn't stop drinking she was going to end their marriage. Pearl had made this threat countless times in their decades of marriage, but now all of the children had launched from the nest and Pearl believed she could afford to live on her own. Buddy was afraid that this time she would go through with leaving him.

Buddy consented to enter an intensive outpatient program at a local hospital. The treatment program included opportunities for family members to attend educational sessions and group meetings to facilitate their understanding of the nature of addiction and its impact on families. Pearl and Buddy continued seeing me for marriage counseling. Addiction treatment and marriage counseling prepared Pearl and Buddy for the adjustments they would face if Buddy remained sober. Sobriety changes family dynamics. The loved ones often don't know how to act except in their old dysfunctional ways. This can become a relapse issue for people in recovery. Armed with information about the challenges of recovery, both of them are now taking it "one day at a time."

* * *

So far in this chapter I have referred to addiction in terms of substance abuse. However, there are countless things a person can be addicted to such as pornography, exercise, Facebook, work, food and gambling. A broad definition of addiction is "anything a person continues to do in spite of negative consequences." An addict often engages in such behavior to avoid unwanted feelings such as sadness, anger or boredom. Some addicts live with so much anxiety that they say they do what they do "to feel normal." There is usually a point at which they do it simply because they are addicted to it.

I describe addiction as a bubble a person crawls into. Within the bubble the addict establishes a reality conceived in their own imagination. It has nothing to do with the real world and yet it seems real to the person who's in the bubble. Usually, the addict draws the family into the bubble to interact in this made-up world. When a family goes into recovery the addict's spouse and the children escape the bubble and all of its distortions and rules. They begin to see how to take care of themselves rather than the addict. It becomes for them a liberation of life-changing proportions!

No one is saying you must dump an addicted spouse. Al-Anon and Nar-Anon groups include people who have chosen to stay with their loved one for whatever reasons. The message I want to leave with you is that no marriage is healthy when a partner is an addict. There is help out there for your mate and for the family.

*   *   *

Another elephant in the living room of millions of families in America is mental illness. Roughly 18% of our population suffers each year from a diagnosable mental illness such as depression, anxiety, schizophrenia or bipolar disorder. The presence of untreated mental disorders can have the same effect on families as addiction, especially the experiences of anger, guilt, shame and silence. Codependency may develop between the family members and the person who is depressed, anxious or delusional. Spouses of the mentally ill are very prone to being in denial about what they are seeing in their mate. Denial about the gravity of the situation often exists in both partners. Men are more likely than women to hide their feelings and to minimize their estimation of the need for treatment.

In America, the suicide rate is nearly 13% per 100,000 people per year. This comes to nearly 113 suicides in our country every single day! It is the second leading cause of death for those from 15-34 years of age. Untreated mental disorders are the major cause of suicide. A man is more likely than a woman to succeed in a suicide attempt. These are hard facts that demand our attention. Please stay observant of your mate's emotional and mental welfare. It could be a matter of life and death.

If your loved one appears to be showing symptoms of mental illness, you must gently encourage him or her to talk to a professional about treatment. For most people the place to start is with your family physician. You may also investigate if there are employee assistance programs in your respective workplaces. An EAP counselor can assess the problem and make appropriate referrals for treatment. You may resort to asking your mate's trusted friend or family member to help you talk them into going for help. As with addiction, the worst thing you can do is to put up a good front to the world about what is really going on in your home. Almost without exception your health insurance will pay for the treatment of mental and emotional problems. There are also non-profit agencies and local government agencies in every county that offer services on a sliding fee-scale based on your income. Some people turn to their church leaders for help. Unfortunately for many folks, their clergy are not well-informed about mental illness and may do more harm than good in their approach to helping. Physicians, licensed psychologists and licensed counselors are your safest sources for assessment and treatment.

Every human being goes through rough patches in their life which bring on some sadness or anxiety. Grief is a natural and normal reaction to losses and changes in one's life. Many people are moody who are not suffering from a diagnosable mental disorder. A person is in red-flag trouble when symptoms develop that keep him or her from functioning well in daily activities and/or that last more than a few weeks. Changes in sleep, appetite and libido are symptoms to watch for as warning signs of illness. If you or your mate has lost your joy in life and your energy level is diminished significantly, it may be depression. Frequent crying spells and thoughts of suicide are real warning signs that something is terribly wrong. It is always better to seek advice regarding such symptoms sooner rather than later.

* * *

Perhaps the most closely guarded secret among American families today is that of domestic violence. The shame one feels after being physically harmed by a loved one or witnessing it is nearly unbearable. Shame is the belief people hold about themselves that says, "There is something wrong, bad, dirty or unacceptable about me." Shame is the most profound silencer of victims. It is made worse by the perpetrator's goal to make the victim feel responsible for what happened in an act of violence. During an assault a husband says, "I wouldn't have to hit you if you'd keep your mouth shut." A wife screams as she slaps her husband, "Do what I say or I'll give you worse than that!" Very often, verbal abuse accompanies physical abuse, deepening the shame.

Early in my career, I was the Director of Abuse Victim Services at a Family Services agency. This included supervising the management of a battered women's shelter and working with the local District Court to enroll batterers in a rehabilitation program. I listened to hundreds of stories told by both victims and perpetrators. From either perspective the person's definition of battering was, as I call it, "the bad thing that hasn't happened yet." A woman who had been slapped would say, "He didn't hit me with his fist." A man who had been kicked would say, "I don't have any broken bones." More than once I met someone for whom the only bad thing that had not happened was death and even then the person was reluctant to admit that they were being abused by a loved one.

According to the National Coalition Against Domestic Violence, 10 million men and women are abused by an intimate partner each year. Every nine seconds in America a woman is beaten or assaulted. Domestic violence is so prevalent in our country that physicians have been instructed to ask their patients during routine exams, "Do you feel safe at home?" Most often, if an assault results in the need for medical care, the victim will lie about how the injury occurred. Violence at home knows no socio-economic, ethnic or religious boundaries. A highly respected member of a community may be a batterer at home.

One tragic result of domestic violence is that it is passed from generation to generation. Children who are victims of violence or who witness it are set up on many levels to become perpetrators or victims of violence as adults. If you are harboring the secret of being battered or verbally abused, it is taking a terrible toll on yours and your children's physical, emotional and mental well-being.

* * *

If you reflect back on your situation you may see that it fits the widely predictable "cycle of violence." It goes like this:

1. One or both partners are feeling a low level of tension at home that goes unresolved.
2. The tension level rises within minutes, hours or days.
3. Both partners begin to feel that the tension is unbearable and yet no effective effort is made to peaceably resolve it.
4. One or both partners consciously or unconsciously starts an argument.
5. Verbal and/or physical violence occurs.
6. Tension is released by the blow-up.
7. Perhaps an apology is made and/ or there is a promise that the violence will never happen again.
8. There is a period of pleasant peace and quiet until…
9. A level of tension rises again.

What is known about this cycle is that most often the assaults become progressively worse over time. Verbal abuse may become physical pushing and shoving, pushing and shoving may become more injurious assaults, etc.

When you love someone who is violent you live in fear. You walk on eggshells trying not to trigger an assault. Violence is the batterer's tool for domination. He or she may know no other way to exercise power and control. If there is not a formal intervention, the cycle of violence at home will not be broken. In almost every county in America there are professionals to turn to who understand domestic violence and how to intervene. Police and sheriff's departments often have officers specially trained to aid victims. There are safe houses one may enter to escape a violent home. Most District Court systems in our country have programs for perpetrators of domestic violence in which they are instructed in anger management and relationship skills in lieu of serving jail time for assault charges.

I have witnessed the effects of professional help being given to victims and abusers. Often the family is reunited and the problem remains under control. For others, a plan to safely leave the relationship is devised and supported by a counselor or an agency. At the very least, I have seen some abuse victims find family or friends to stay with during a period of heightened threat. The downside of that is the one who takes you in could be in peril if the violent person seeks you at their home. Safety should always be the first consideration.

Clearly, dealing with domestic violence can be a dangerous and complicated matter that needs to be handled with wisdom and careful planning. But it surely should not be covered up and allowed to fester. No one deserves to live like that.

Elephants in the living room don't usually go away with time. If you love someone who is an addict, is suffering the symptoms of mental or emotional distress, or is verbally and/or physically violent, you also are deeply impacted by their problems. If you are committed to your mate for a lifetime, part of your commitment is to give them support in times of need. Sometimes that support must be augmented by bringing their disorder out in the open and letting family, friends and professionals join you in helping them to get well. Seek help. No more secrets!

CHAPTER 10

Your People Will Be My People

Perhaps the least expected marital discord you will encounter is the one that arises around in-laws. When you marry your mate, you marry his or her family, too. Don't let anyone tell you any differently. This is true even if every one of those family members is deceased. Just remember that almost every aspect of your mate was and is profoundly influenced by family relationships. In person or as phantoms you will live with these people throughout your marriage.

I want to start by saying that my in-laws were the kindest family I could've ever asked for to "be my people." My mother-in-law would bake a pie just for me when I went to visit them. They never tried to give advice or interfere in any way. I counted my blessings in the in-law department. Les and Arlene are now deceased but I wish you could have met them and observed the very best models for extended family relationships.

There is a Biblical reference to the notion that two people should leave their respective families and "cleave" to one another. Cleave meant they would stick together. This "leave and cleave" concept in American culture is generally accepted as a good idea, but in reality many couples find themselves unable to fully achieve it. There is often one (sometimes both) spouse who never really "left the nest" when the marriage was formed. I have counseled many men and women who have complained that their mate is still very attached to and dependent on his or her parent(s).

This dependency can be blatantly obvious as in when a man visits his mother several times a week, often to perform some helpful task for her or to have her cook for him. Or a woman may talk to her mother several times each day or for an hour several times each week. These visits and calls would be considered dysfunctional mostly because it takes time away from the person's immediate family. Mom and Dad are getting too much time and attention from their adult child who probably has little free time to spend with his or her mate and children. Unless your parents are unwell and need extra caretaking, you do not want your mate to consistently feel that you put your parents first on your priority list.

Many couples tell me their parents are the initiators of excessive amounts of contact. They report that a parent calls many times a week or drops in frequently without being invited. It is vital for limits on these behaviors to be set in the *very beginning* of a marriage. It is much easier to establish good boundaries with parents and in-laws from day one. It is painful and difficult to try to ask for privacy later on after the precedent of an "open door" has been set. However, sometimes the inappropriate intrusions begin when the first grandchild is born. This would call for limits to be set at that time.

Please note that I am not saying closeness and visits with parents are necessarily harmful to a couple's marriage. The problem lies in the ratio of time and energy you spend with other family members besides your mate and children. Your parents have to adjust to your having a life with the family you've created through marriage. They must learn to play a collateral role in your life instead of primary. This shift is very difficult for many parents to abide especially if you expect them to help you when you need them and to leave you alone when you don't.

Besides spending too much time visiting and/or talking on the phone with your parents, another indicator that you have not fully "left home" is when your parents know way too much about the personal details of your marriage. Your parents are not supposed to be "all up in your business." There needs to be a "sacred space" of privacy with your partner to which your parents have absolutely no access.

One of the worst things a marital partner can do is go to the parents for sympathy and/or advice when a conflict has occurred in the marriage. You have to know that long after you and your mate have kissed and made up, your parents will remember all the bad things you told them. In their eyes your mate has "hurt their baby" and they could hold a grudge about that until they die. It is a rare parent who would be objective about your marital conflicts. This is especially true if your mate has been unfaithful.

* * *

One unfortunate wa parents can be too involved in their child's life is when they are giving their son or daughter money. It has not been a good trend in American culture for parents of any socio-economic class to bail out their adult children when the children overspend or get in trouble. Some parents have even put up bail or paid lawyers' fees by mortgaging their houses when their adult child commits a crime. There are moms and dads who have repeatedly paid off their kids' credit card balances. Receiving help from your parents in the dire circumstances of your life is not in itself dysfunctional. It is dysfunctional when their financial help enables you to keep making the same bad choices over and over again. It is a destructive type of codependency when your parents soften all the blows in your life with their money.

* * *

There is a longstanding stereotype of a mother-in-law being jealous of her son's relationship with his wife. Trying to monopolize her son's time is one way to get "one up" on her daughter-in-law, and/or she may be hyper-critical of her. A mother-in-law may be shamelessly open with her criticism of a son or daughter-in-law while others make more subtle jabs. If your parent is in any way trying to win in a power struggle with your mate, the person who can put a stop to it is *you*.

William knew when he married Tess that his mother was having a hard time sharing him with his new wife. His mom loved him dearly and stayed in constant contact with him all of his life. She had conveyed to him, as he approached adulthood, that there was probably not anyone out there who could take care of him like she does. She was never warm and accepting to his girlfriends. She would find fault with every one of them. Tess was no exception.

William never challenged his mother's criticism of the girls he dated. He maintained denial about his mother's possessiveness. When he fell in love with Tess, he thought his mother would just get used to the idea that he was directing his life primarily towards Tess and their marriage. Instead of acclimating to William's focus on his marriage, Mom doubled her efforts to control him with demands and guilt trips. Tess's resentment of her mother-in-law was a growing poison in her relationship with William. She was hurt and angry that William did not take up for her and set limits by confronting Mom about her behaviors.

* * *

Christie grew up as a "daddy's girl." She and her father shared a close relationship through doing fun things together and talking daily about the little and big things in Christie's life. She admired and trusted her father and sought his help and advice well into her adult life. She always thought she wanted to marry a man "just like Dad." When she met Gabriel she thought she had found a guy as special as her father.

Gabriel liked his father-in-law well enough. He simply felt that Christie went to her father first when she needed something or wanted to talk through a problem. She knew Dad would be there in a minute if she asked him to fix the toilet or loan her money. Dad was glad to take her to lunch and listen to her complaints about Gabriel or life in general. Gabriel began to believe that Christie trusted her father more than she trusted him and he felt unneeded in their relationship.

As with William and Christie, when one partner in a marriage fails to truly leave the parents and cleave to his or her mate, the mate eventually feels that the marital love, trust and respect is diminished. Every man or woman wants to feel *most* special to his or her spouse. Never achieving independence from your parents casts a shadow over the intimacy in your marriage. I have asked couples in counseling, "Who do you call first with big news?" If your honest answer would be "my parents," then there is a problem with your priorities. Tess and Gabriel resented not being "number one" and those marriages were at risk of failure.

I often hear from couples that one or both sets of in-laws began creating conflicts when the grandchildren were born. The most frequently cited conflict involves holidays and other special occasions such as birthdays. It seems all the relatives want the "prime time." Some of the worst guilt trips you can experience can be laid on you by your folks who want you at their house when the kids open their presents. To reiterate, the solution to this dilemma lies in setting precedents *right away* as to how you two plan to handle family expectations regarding visits. (Again: Expectations are resentments waiting to happen.) Bringing your children to visit their grandparents should almost always be on *your* terms.

I realize it is excruciating to be the one to break a family tradition. "But we've always gone to Grandma's for Thanksgiving!" exclaims your mother when you tell her that you and your partner plan to do otherwise this year. It is even worse for you to have to handle the hard feelings of your parents when you actually like your family's traditions and you don't really want to give them up. Many couples dread every holiday season because of these sticky situations. I usually suggest that a newlywed couple establish their own new ways of celebrating special occasions *in their own home.* This will probably necessitate arranging a trip to the in-laws' homes before or after the actual holiday or birthday. Lots of couples solve the problem with holiday visits by alternating years with each other's families. This is an especially helpful solution when one or both sets of in-laws live a long distance away because the distance prohibits the "we'll go to your mom's house for lunch and to mine for supper" compromise.

* * *

A couple really has to support each other emotionally when challenges to family traditions are being made. You have to help each other work through the inevitable guilt that comes with disappointing your loved ones. Just remember there may be initial negative reactions, even emotional punishment, from your respective parents when you don't do what they want. However, if you stand your ground, your families will eventually adjust to the changes and learn to accept what you've proposed as the compromises. It is vital that your parents are convinced by the two of you that your proposal is what *both of you* want and agree on. Otherwise your parents will blame your spouse for the changes and possibly never forgive him or her for it.

Couples with children come to me with the complaint that their parents do not respect their wishes regarding how the grandkids should be treated. In-laws often have their own beliefs about discipline, food, sleep, manners and religious upbringing, just to name a few. How often do you hear someone say, "Those children are spoiled rotten by their Mimi and Papa?" It is really tricky to find the comfortable ground between your parental authority and the natural tendency for most grandparents to indulge their grandchildren in spite of your rules or to be harsh with the kids about things you feel are not a big deal.

You really must ask grandparents to respect your *most basic* rules regarding your children. Those rules usually cover such things as their sleep routine, their safety and their manners towards adults and peers. If a grandparent gets out of line with the grandchildren, it is the place of the *biological child* of those grandparents to address the issue with them. Infractions need to be dealt with immediately and firmly. Set the precedents of what you expect starting with the birth of your first child. This will eliminate awkward and difficult discussions becoming necessary later when you've put up with it until you explode.

Do try to leave a lot of latitude for the in-laws to love the grandchildren in their own inimitable way. Most of us who had the blessing of knowing our grandparents can remember a distinct way they showed love for us. My grandmothers were both good cooks who nurtured their loved ones with food. My parents never put any restrictions on that and getting to eat lots of wonderful things is a happy memory for me.

* * *

Unfortunately, there is an in-law topic that must be addressed. Some of us have a toxic parent who will also be a toxic in-law and a toxic grandparent. To label a parent as "toxic" is measured by the degree of negative influence the parent imposes on the people around him or her. Such negativity can be the result of addiction, personality disorder and/or inadequately treated mental illness, among other things. It could be the parent has been verbally, physically and/or sexually abusive to you or your siblings as you grew up. Some people are toxic mainly because they always find a way to create chaos and stir up trouble wherever they go.

It is your solemn duty to protect your children from a toxic grandparent. If the children do spend time with this grandparent it must *always*, without exception, be on your terms and under your watchful supervision. I am dumfounded by the number of people I have met who have a terrible history with one or both parents and yet will leave their children with those parents unsupervised!

Evidently, it is human nature to be in denial that what a parent has done to you will be done to your children, too. It is a sad statistic that most children who are molested are harmed by someone they know, often a family member. Most sexually inappropriate adults do not "reform" simply by growing older. More than one parent has admitted to me that their child's grandparent was caught introducing the child to sex through internet pornography or R-rated movies. You must pay attention to your history with your parents and/or to any queasy feelings you get about your children's interactions with their grandparents or other relatives. Too many parents are afraid of hurting someone's feelings or stirring up family conflict by challenging grandparents' behaviors. Just remember that if you don't protect your children no one will!

I am not saying that if your mother or father was less than stellar as your parent they can't be good grandparents. Sexual abuse is one thing, but poor parenting practices are another. Perhaps your parents were ignorant or immature in their raising of you but have gotten older and wiser and mellower as the years went by. Just keep a watchful eye on your parents and your in-law's interactions with your children and see how the trends develop instead of assuming the worst. Letting your expectations be clear and setting limits early on will be your best strategy for establishing guidelines with grandparents. If they disrespect these guidelines they may be proving that they will be no better at being grandparents than they were at parenting you.

Don't be surprised if your children prefer one set of grandparents over another. It often happens. Try not to let this influence you to shut out the less preferred grandparents from visits and family celebrations. If you can, discover what is at the root of your children's feelings. There might be ways to address the situation by advising the grandparents of different ways to interact with the grandchildren. Lead your children by example in showing love and respect to all their relatives. You should always require your children to be well-mannered and to show appreciation when at grandma and grandpa's house.

Relating to the older generation in your family can be a delicate balance of showing them love and respect while maintaining boundaries to protect your marriage and your children from inappropriate behavior. Guilt or financial manipulations will hopefully never be a factor in your relationships. In the best of circumstances, your parents and in-laws will be abundant sources of emotional support and even wisdom as you face life's challenges together. As they say, "What goes around comes around," and your children are watching.

CHAPTER 11

The Cost of Money

Ralph Waldo Emerson wrote, "Money often costs too much." Sometimes it costs a couple their marriage. Well over 30% of divorced couples in America would say money issues broke up their marriage and I believe the vast majority of all couples would say they've had humdinger arguments over it. Sonya Britt, a Kansas State University researcher, says arguing about money is the number one predictor of divorce regardless of the couple's socioeconomic status. Other research has shown that the more often a couple argues about money, the higher the risk of divorce. Money is a hot topic in marriage that can flame out of control!

Money was certainly a problem early in my relationship with my mate. I partnered with a person who had already learned how to manage money very well. I had not. I was of the mind, "I must have money. I still have checks!" I spent money when I got it and only the bank knew how much was in my account most weeks. My shopping was "retail therapy." I loved the thrill of the hunt for a "great bargain."

I would come home with my newest purchase bragging about how much I had saved. My partner was unimpressed. Instead of, "Great!" I heard, "You didn't save money if you spent it." It was constantly pointed out that I was reaching middle age and had not saved much of anything from my income over the years. Because I was self-employed for most of my adult life, there was no employer funded IRA or 401-K. I was one medical crisis away from bankruptcy and had never thought about it. Yes, I was that dumb.

I am eternally grateful to my mate for forcing me to think about, discuss and make plans for my/our money. After we joined our lives together I started putting money in a retirement fund and keeping a small savings account. It wasn't fair to expect my mate to bear all the burden of a financial crisis if we had one. I also stopped shopping so much. That was the hardest part, and still is.

I have made the case in this book that most people marry their opposite. This tends to be true regarding money management. Spenders marry savers and impulse buyers marry planners who generally don't like to shop. When you were thinking of making a life together with your mate, I hope you considered whether or not you share the same "core values" even if your spending styles differ. You are likely to be in deep conflict if you don't agree on what you spend for and invest in.

The spending and saving of money usually reflects what a person thinks is important in life. Couples get along better if their financial decisions flow from a common view of things like charity, lifestyle and having a comfortable retirement. Even if greed is your family value, you get along better if you are both greedy. My mate and I have grown to understand that we value travel above almost any other expenditure. We believe experiences are more precious than things. For some couples a priority is saving for their children's education. For others it is pursuing status symbols of wealth, even if they aren't particularly wealthy. I have met many folks who appear to be "living the life" but were actually deeply in debt.

People misquote the Bible when they say, "Money is the root of all evil." The scripture actually says, "The *love* of money is the root of all evil." Perhaps the love of *things* is the root of all evil. I believe credit cards are a root of evil for millions of people! I learned to stop asking couples if they are in credit card debt. I just started asking,

"How much credit card debt do you have?" Often the answer is in the tens of thousands. Add to that their car payments and mortgages and it is easy to see why couples of all socio-economic levels worry about money.

Typically, one partner worries about money more than the other one does. These worries are not generally rationally discussed. They erupt to the surface in arguments but are never effectively addressed. Money problems are a festering sore in many marriages. Interestingly, family financial concerns are rarely the presenting problem when a couple seeks marriage counseling. However, it doesn't take long for the conflicts surrounding money to be brought up in sessions.

In most families there is usually one person who keeps track of paying the bills. That spouse is often the one who worries about the money because of the first-hand knowledge of how much is going out compared to what is coming in. This person is also the one who may hide money problems from their mate for a variety of reasons.

* * *

I had worked with Barbie and Noah for quite a while when Barbie called me to say she had a big problem to bring up in our session and wanted me to be prepared for "all hell to break loose." In the session she confessed to Noah and me that their savings, which Noah believed to hold nearly $17,000.00, was completely gone. Barbie had been using it for months to make ends meet. Barbie really feared that physical violence would happen in response to this news. It was not easy to calm Noah down enough to proceed in using the session to figure out how he could deal with his anger and Barbie's fear.

It is probably no surprise that this marriage didn't make it. Not because of that particular loss of money but because this disaster revealed how poorly they communicated and how low their level of trust had become. I have found that when one partner lies about or hides money it may affect the other partner's trust as profoundly as would sexual infidelity. Unfortunately, scenarios such as Barbie and Noah's happen every day in our culture. Lack of honest communication about money ultimately causes a great deal of anxiety, distrust and anger and, as with Barbie and Noah, will likely contribute to the destruction of the relationship.

* * *

As you examine the role of money in your marriage, you may want to begin with your family of origin's history with money. Do you come from generations of poverty or of wealth? As you grew up did you feel deprived of things you needed or wanted or did you take for granted that if you asked for something you got it? How did your parents handle their finances? Did you ever receive instructions about how to manage money and save it? Do you look at some possible inheritance from the older generation as your "safety" fund for retirement? Our emotional, intellectual and social relationship with money probably starts before we are five years old and we bring that relationship with money into our marriage.

There are currently serious questions about the future solvency of the Social Security program in America. Companies are eliminating pension programs and reducing retirement and health care contributions. Taking on more and more of our health care costs has greatly reduced our funds for other monthly expenses. The costs of a college education have skyrocketed. Children feel entitled to their parents paying for their very expensive weddings and even helping with their first mortgage down-payment. Auto maintenance and repair costs can drain a bank account even if you have insurance. You would think that with these issues impacting our finances we would all be very, very careful about saving for the future. It would make sense for every couple to have developed a budget with a commitment to honor it. Instead, people decide to leave things to chance and bail themselves out with credit cards when they come up short. Your emotional relationship with money affects such decisions for better or worse.

No one could say that very many couples today exercise common sense when it comes to handling finances. Rarely has a couple answered yes to my inquiry as to whether they have *actually written out* a budget plan. Almost without exception, my question is met with a clearing of the throat and a murmur of, "Not exactly. We've been meaning to do it but we haven't done it yet." This comes from folks who have been together for anywhere from one year to forty years. Invariably, one mate blames the other for the reluctance to sit down and discuss money and get financial plans on paper.

One of you must take the leadership to talk about financial plans. When it comes to your family money, ignorance is not bliss. If you need help with assessing your status and making a viable plan there are countless resources available. Some churches offer Dave Ramsey's courses on money management. PBS has offered Suze Orman's books and videos during fundraising seasons. There are online courses, IPhone apps and financial advisors galore available to get you on the right track.

Many reputable financial advisors have products to sell and charge a fee for buying and selling investments. There are also mutual fund companies such as Vanguard, Fidelity and T. Rowe Price (a Google search will turn up options and consumer reviews of these) with whom you can do business directly for a minimal fund management fee. Investments made in these ways are generally done in addition to your employer's 401-K plan. I see couples who think nothing of borrowing money from their 401-K to catch up on their bills. That is why I think having separate investments from your retirement plan is a good idea because you do not want to gamble with the money you will someday rely on for living expenses.

Regarding using financial advisors, you may want to go to a "fee only" financial planner with whom you can look at your situation, make changes, set goals and gain confidence about your future prospects. Fee only advisors do not sell products so you won't be coaxed into questionable investments. Some part of the fee is tax deductible. Whatever you do, you absolutely must check out the established credentials and reputation of your advisors. There's always someone out there who will commit fraud or lead you into poor investments and unnecessary risks.

*　*　*

The basics of family money management lie in the open, honest communication between you and your partner about what is coming in and what is going out. I have already mentioned what happens when one partner lies about or hides money from the other. This sometimes happens in the form of a spouse hiding expenditures from the other or of maintaining a "secret stash" of savings for personal use. Unfortunately, deceptions about money are most likely to happen when one of you doesn't participate in the overseeing of family finances.

If you lost your mate tomorrow, would you know where all the money is? Do you have access to account numbers and passwords? Do you even know how many accounts you have as a couple and as individuals? Sadly, many couples haven't even made wills that assign the particulars of the settlement of their joint estate. What you don't know *can hurt you* both now and in the future.

At our house, we have a bowl on top of the refrigerator into which we put every single receipt we get. My partner is a charts and graphs kind of person and is willing to plug those receipts into categories of spending. There are websites such as Mint.com that will help you with this if neither of you is interested in setting it up. By recording the receipts, we know where our money has gone by the end of the month. We break down our once-a-year payments such as taxes and insurance into 12- month increments. These along with utilities and other recurring monthly fees are added to grocery, entertainment and miscellaneous receipts. This chart helps us see how much we spend regularly and thus see how much we have left over to put into savings. We also have earmarked funds for things like our annual vacation, new furniture and household improvements. With this attention to details, we very rarely experience financial situations we would have to go into debt to handle.

Most financial experts tell us it is prudent to keep up to one year's worth of income in an accessible emergency fund. Many couples I counsel have less than $1,000.00 in accessible savings. It seems that regardless of income level people spend what they make (or more!). This practice of spending rather than saving has led to far too many families filing bankruptcy at least once. Poor planning for emergencies, credit card debt and reckless spending usually result in financial trouble. In the near future, the burden of student loan debt will be a culprit in ruining the finances in many households. A frightening number of couples in our country are oblivious to how devastating a health care crisis could be to their savings. Some very smart people can be very dumb about money.

Brene Brown said, "Comparison is the thief of happiness." In our culture, we are happier if we think we have more than our neighbors. However, most of us believe that others have more than we do. We strive to at least keep up the appearance of having what others have, even if we go deeply into debt to do so. In 2016, the poverty level for a family of four is $22,811.00. The working poor struggle with decisions about what bills to pay, what food to buy and what medical care to seek. Are you comparing your finances to theirs or to the conspicuous consumers you meet everywhere you go? Researchers have found that, for an average person's needs, a $75,000.00 annual income is sufficient for happiness and no amount of income above that significantly increased the report of happiness by responders to the survey. So, life can get "comfortable" at a certain level of income if you handle your money well. If you don't handle your money well, misery will abide with you no matter what your salary is.

* * *

In marriage, money can be a means of control. Hopefully you are not experiencing a power struggle based on who holds the purse strings. A stay-at-home parent is sometimes subject to this dilemma. Not having an independent income may keep you tied to a spouse who barely allows you the money for household expenses. I have seen couples on the verge of divorce because the income earner dictated everything about family life based on how he or she wanted the money to be spent. The doling out of money can be a means of manipulation and the withholding of money becomes a spiteful punishment.

When there is only one wage earner in a family, even *more* communication and planning about money is vital to the health of the relationship. Talking about spending and saving as *equal partners* helps to prevent the use of money as a control factor by one spouse over the other. Often, the working parent is the husband. The wife buys the groceries, the clothes and other necessities for the children and all the things that keep the household running using only an "allowance" of monthly funds supplied by her husband. I have frequently heard the complaint that the husband is out of touch regarding the current cost of things like food, medical services and sports participation fees. He complains about how much his wife spends and they argue about it. Looking at real expenses together every month helps to minimize these conflicts and can facilitate more realistic financial plans.

Remember, as with all the subjects covered in this book, the best way to have a happy marriage is to have fun and share emotional support. Money is a means to both those ends. Handling finances will be one of the most intentional and purposeful things you will do together. Don't let anxiety or ignorance stop you from establishing this powerful basis of security in your relationship.

CHAPTER 12

The 30 Year Tune-Up

The author of Ecclesiastes wrote, "To everything there is a season, and a time to every purpose under heaven: a time to be born and a time to die, a time to plant and a time to pluck up that which is planted;...a time to weep and a time to laugh, a time to mourn and a time to dance." These cycles exist in marriage and family life as surely as we draw breath. Throughout the chapters of this book I have made reference to the many stages of marriage and family life starting with the chemistry and psychology of attraction. Ah, remember those first thrills of excitement which evolved into the "urge to merge?" The tingles associated with PEA coursing through your brain eventually gave way to a deeper, quieter and more reliable love. This was the season of leaving your parents or your already established independent life and "cleaving" to a mate. You promised to spend a lifetime together. In those days, you might not have had financial wealth but you were rich in love.

It is usually soon after the falling-in-love season of your relationship that the season for establishing the foundation of your life together begins. You have your children and choose your careers. You buy your first house and maybe a minivan. This season is a time of living as partners more side-to-side than face-to-face. Your partnership meets the demands of raising children and working, but it may rarely include time alone together fostering intimacy. Your energies are spent in a myriad of ways, giving to almost anyone or anything else but each other. This season lasts well into your children's teenage years. It is when many couples report losing their feelings of closeness and interest in each other. The marriage nearly dies of neglect if the couple is not conscious and intentional about maintaining their bond. It is interesting that lots of couples feel pretty content with life during this season. They are enjoying the rewards of raising the children and thriving in their careers. They don't necessarily miss the marital intimacy that is slipping away.

Because the feelings of closeness are not being carefully maintained, the marriage is vulnerable to infidelity during those years. Having the charming attention of another adult is flattering and seductive when things have grown stale at home. When counselors see couples who are in this season of marriage, a popular piece of advice is "Go on regular dates. Spend time together without the children or other intrusions." In my chapter on The Huddle I explained an effective way to regularly make time for each other in spite of the hectic, activity-filled days that are pulling you in opposite directions. Being thoughtful and careful during these nearly two decades can overcome the perils that come with this season of married life.

Midlife for both men and women presents new challenges in almost every area of their lives. Body, mind and spirit. It is a season of asking yourself, "Is my life what I had hoped it would be by now? Have I accomplished my goals? Have my dreams come true?" It can be a time of unfavorably comparing yourself to your peers even though you probably don't know the full story of their lives. Your body is aging, your memory isn't what it used to be and your energy doesn't serve you like it did in your 20's and 30's. You've probably had grave challenges to your faith in God and in humanity by midlife. You may start to panic about saving enough money for retirement. It can all be a bit too much to handle gracefully.

In this middle season, your children have become busy and often insulting as they establish their independence. You are trying to guide them through the demands and pressures of their adolescence while also interacting with or caring for aging parents. Some refer to this as the "sandwich season" of life due to your having to give attention to both your children and your parents in simultaneously occurring situations. You are caught in the middle of the needs of your loved ones. It is often exhausting.

This season also ushers in "the change" for women. The approach of menopause brings physical, mental and emotional transformations that can wreak havoc with their sexual desire and ability to have pain free, pleasurable intercourse. With each decade after age 40, men may begin to experience some loss of sexual energy and may develop erectile dysfunction to some degree. If these sexual changes during the midlife season of marriage aren't handled with love, empathy and thoughtfulness they may drive an emotional wedge between marital partners.

Our 40's and 50's are generally hectic and fraught with layers of complex changes on every front. In a good marriage, a couple will turn to each to each other for support as co-captains of "team family" and weather it all with affection and humor. Unfortunately, many couples become ships passing in the night and live as roommates as they co-parent their children.

When the Empty Nest becomes the new normal for the household it forces a couple to assess the quality of their relationship. In 21st century America, this has become a time for many marriages to break up. I believe divorces in this season of life could be avoided by having a "30 year tune-up" done with a skilled marriage counselor. Some of my favorite work is with couples who are entering what I call the "companionship season" of their marriage. The 30 year tune-up can set the course for a couple's next three decades together.

* * *

Luke and Margo Busby said a tearful good-bye to their youngest child, Dustin, as they walked out of his new abode, the college residence hall. It was a quiet ride home. Luke was thinking "I'm going to have to work until I am 75 to pay for Dustin's tuition." Margo was thinking "Now what? The kids are away from home and I'm not sure how I want to spend my time outside of working at the bank." Margo looked over at Luke and wondered "Do I know this man?" The Busbys are facing the years ahead knowing that life as they have known it for over two decades is going to change forever. They will consider questions about when and how to retire from their careers, how much money they should be saving, how to foster good health, will they downsize their home and who is going to take care of their elderly parents. I have spent many hours with folks, mostly women, who are asking themselves regarding their spouse, "Am I better off with him or without him?" So many people stay with their mate for the sake of the children and they don't ask this question until the kids leave home. When your last child has reached adulthood, leaving the marriage becomes an option especially if you can financially afford a divorce. The book "Too Good to Leave, Too Bad to Stay" has been a helpful resource to my clients in making a decision about divorce. Unless they are certain they want out of the marriage, I usually urge an unhappy client to not give up without trying to bring in his or her mate to discuss staying together.

Because I believe that couples mostly want to feel supported and have fun in their marriage, we have to focus our sessions on finding ways for them to have what they desire. Sometimes their history together is so negative and painful there is no simple or predictably successful way to bounce back from the sorrow and bitterness. "A death by a thousand cuts" is the way I describe the demise of their relationship. It is not usually one or two big things that irreparably harm a marriage. It is more often an accumulation of hurts, disappointments and/or neglect that finally crushes it. Saving such a deeply wounded marriage involves honesty, patience and lots of forgiveness. We cannot get far with marriage counseling if one mate is saying, "I'm over all that bad stuff, why aren't you?" There has to be no more silence, denial and sweeping things under the rug. We can't sew up wounds without disinfecting them. It takes courage and commitment to hang tough through these sessions. But I have seen some miraculous results.

* * *

Not all couples who seek a 30 year tune-up arrive with a lot of negative baggage to unpack. That was true of Luke and Margo Busby. They simply wanted to strengthen the foundation of their marriage so they could face the future securely and pleasantly. I describe this process as "negotiating a new contract." Such negotiations happen in one's career as the corporate ladder is ascended. Why not see it as a valuable endeavor in a marriage? For partners like the Busbys who just want a tune-up, I start the contract negotiation with a session of serious reflection on the current qualities of the relationship. I hand each mate a pen and memo pad and tell them to make three columns. In regard to their marriage:

1. What do you want to get rid of?
2. What do you want to keep?
3. What do you want to add?

Discussing these points can sometimes take several sessions. I love it when I see the couple smile as they remember what is still good between them. This softens the impact of talking about what to get rid of. Almost every couple says they want to add better communication and more fun time together. Some couples want to revive their sex life. After we have clearly established the new contract as a guideline for future behaviors, we can use the ideas I've shared in this book to beef up their marriage skills. Seeking this type of relationship counseling can save your marriage and actually make it possible to have a "new and improved" relationship. After only a few sessions Luke and Margo Busby felt they had the tools to spruce up their dull marriage and were ready to enter their companionship season with hope for very good times ahead.

Staying together for at least 50 years doesn't mean hanging in there, accepting the same old unhealthy, ineffective interaction patterns. Who wants to simply endure a marriage? Especially when the last season of your life together often requires the devoted caretaking of each other in your infirmities. It is ideal for you to enter old age together having had a decade or two of great companionship and deep bonding. It is seldom too late to improve a marriage and make your relationship dreams come true. Why not get started now?

Wouldn't it be wonderful if a book, CD or video providing helpful advice about maintaining a good relationship could be given out with every marriage license? What would happen to the quality of family life in America if every adult had to take a marriage license renewal test every few years like we do to renew our driver's license? Dear readers, knowledge is power. I hope that reading "Staying Together for At Least 50 Years" has given you the power to have the marriage you want 'til death do you part.

References

Auerbach, Jeff. *Irritating the Ones You Love.* Cedar Fort, 2002.

Beattie, Melody. *Codependent No More.* Hazelden, 1992.

Brown, Brene´. *The Gifts of Imperfection.* Hazelden, 2010.

Chapman, Gary. *The Five Love Languages.* Northfield Publishing, 2015.

Chapman, Gary and Jennifer Thomas. *The Five Languages of Apology.* Northfield Publishing, 2006.

Fertel, Mort. *Marriage Fitness.* Marriage Max, Inc., 2004.

Gottman, John. *The Seven Principles for Making Marriage Work.* Crown Publishers, 1999.

Hendrix, Harville. *Getting the Love You Want.* Henry Holt and Company, 1988.

Johnson, Sue. *Hold Me Tight.* Little, Brown and Company, 2008.

Kirshenbaum, Mira. *Too Good to Leave, Too Bad to Stay.* Plume, 1997.

Lerner, Harriet. *The Dance of Intimacy.* Harper Perennial, 1990.

Lerner, Harriet. *The Dance of Anger.* William Morrow, 2014.

Littauer, Florence. *After Every Wedding Comes a Marriage.* Harvest House Publishers, 1997

Littauer, Marita. *Wired That Way: The Comprehensive Personality Plan.* Revell, 2006.

Love, Patricia and Steven Stosney. *How to Improve Your Marriage without Talking About It.* Three Rivers Press, 2007.

McCarthy, Barry. *Rekindling Desire*. Routledge, 2013.
Spring, Janis. *After the Affair, 2nd Edition*. William Morrow, 2012.
Szalavitz, Maia. *The Unbroken Brain*. St. Martin's Press. 2016.
www.bettermarriages.org

Acknowledgements

I would have lost almost every word of this book while typing it if it had not been for the computer skills of my very knowledgeable partner in life, Kathleen, who could retrieve all the writing I lost to the ether of cyberspace each time I hit a wrong button. Countless times she dried my tears of frustration and hopelessness and encouraged me to soldier on to finish all the chapters and find a way to get published. Mere words cannot express my gratitude for her support.

My editor, Ellen LaConte, has been the soul of kindness in providing feedback about needed changes and additions. She helped me believe I had something worthwhile to say and she helped me say it so you could enjoy it. I can hardly believe how lucky I am to have found her right when I needed her.

I deeply appreciate my friends and family who read chapters and made suggestions along the way. Thank you Jack Scruggs, Joy Marcum, William Durham, Zack Parmer, Vicki Carr and Priscilla Hunt for contributing your time and effort.

I also want to thank all the folks who have entrusted me with their most guarded secrets and deepest pain. It has been an honor and a privilege to have the opportunity to help you. Sometimes I've gotten to see you years after you sought counseling with me and learned that the rest of the story turned out well. This brings me more joy than I can say.

In my 61 years of enjoying the friendship of some of the most wonderful people who ever walked this planet, I have been close to married couples who were truly happy. Their example of what it means to love and be loved has ever remained an inspiration to me. Here's to all my dear ones who have stayed together for at least 50 years!

About the Author

ynn Parsley, MA, LPC has been an educator and counselor working with individuals, couples and families for nearly forty years. She is a member of the American Association of Marriage and Family Therapists. This book is a distillation of thousands of hours of listening to and learning from people facing the challenges of marriage and family life. With humor and wisdom Lynn addresses the four main conflict issues in marriages as well as other hot topics.

Lynn resides and maintains a private practice in Winston-Salem, North Carolina.

96912194R00075

Made in the USA
Columbia, SC
05 June 2018